Alastair Brian Atkin spent an idyllic early childhood in his family village on the then largely unspoilt Lincolnshire coast. Following bleak wartime and post war years in the middle of the Fens at Spalding, he went on to London University. After National Service as an R.A.F. Officer, he then spent the next thirty-seven challenging years as a professional engineer in the oil/petrochemical industry, being awarded the M.B.E. for services to the same in 1990.

Since retirement he and his wife have lived on Exmoor, their favourite walking area. They have two sons and a daughter, all keen walkers, and seven grandchildren.

Brian has previously written three walking guides and numerous magazine articles.

A
WALKING LIFE

ALASTAIR BRIAN ATKIN

A Walking Life

Vanguard Press

VANGUARD PAPERBACK

A CIP catalogue record for this title is
available from the British Library
ISBN 1 84386 119 4

*Vanguard Press is an imprint of
Pegasus Elliot MacKenzie Publishers Ltd.*
www.pegasuspublishers.com

First Published in 2004

**Vanguard Press
Sheraton House Castle Park
Cambridge England**

Printed & Bound in Great Britain

Dedication

To all my walking companions
over the years.

Especially to Sunya, Gavin, Lindsay and
Matthew, my close family members.

Contents

INTRODUCTION

Sometimes I think my lifelong passion for walking has a great deal to do with an early idyllic environment and at others that I came into this world already designed and programmed to walk in the countryside. In support of the second hypothesis, I have to say that my father and both my grandfathers all had wanderlust in their veins, although I was the only member of the quartet who took to wandering on foot.

During my early walking days, I sometimes wondered whether this strong affinity might be a cause for concern. At that period the number of active walkers in the general population, especially the younger part, was very small and because walking had come to be regarded as a rather oddball activity, it seemed that my passion might mean that I too was odd. However, time has shown that society at that period, totally consumed by materialism after recent wartime and post war shortages, was itself unusual.

The reason why so many modern people feel the need to leave their urban homes behind and explore the countryside has roots deep in our psyche. Our genes are shaped by countless generations of ancestors, the great majority of whom lived wandering outdoor lives, a pattern that only changed when man began farming. The ancient world was a very harsh one and to survive individuals had to be closely attuned to their outdoor surroundings. Through their genes the survivors passed this talent on to their descendants, and subsequently on to us in spite of some blunting during the period since farming began. In the modern world this ancient talent still needs satisfaction and today it is achieved through outdoor recreation, especially in the form of country walking.

Turning to history's shorter term, a single life is only a drop in the ocean of time, but within mine there have been great changes to man's world and also to the natural one. There is a truism that the past is another country and this emerges from the following pages describing the freedom, challenges, friendships, joys, humour, rare fears, occasional sadness and, most important of all, the wonders of the great outdoors. My only regret is that life can never be long enough to take advantage of all that is on offer.

This account, mostly based on contemporary journals, describes my walking experiences in a wide variety of scenes and weathers from the early 1930's up to the present day.

CHAPTER ONE

IDYLL

My first ten years had a major impact on later life. In those days Chapel St. Leonards was a small but growing village on Lincolnshire's North Sea coast some seven miles north of Skegness. Above the sandy gently sloping beach, narrow at high tide and wide at low, a prominent line of sand dunes marked the true beginning of the land. Covered mainly by marram grass, buckthorn and secret bushy dells, these were known locally as the Sand Hills. Inland, flat but uneven ground stretched away for several miles before climbing slowly up to the chalk Lincolnshire Wolds. The last remained a terra incognita throughout my early days.

The village was then a scattered settlement, the remnants of a larger one which had succumbed to the sea in the late sixteenth century. With a mix of plain red brick cottages and recent cheaply-built bungalows, often with colonial style verandas, it would not have made a particularly attractive scene for adult eyes. However, the young had no aesthetic taste because their small home village was their total universe and here the sea, the beach and the Sand Hills all played major roles. The first, often serene but sometimes raging, gave us a first insight to the massive powers of nature. Later, on learning to read, we discovered that this same water led away to exotic distant places where pirates had once roamed. Next came the golden sand, sea shells and fascinating pebbles of the beach which extended both north and south until disappearing out of sight. Finally, the Sand Hills, with their intimate bushy dens and remains of pill boxes, made ideal settings for our make believe games. Later, we learnt that the latter had been built during the Great War when a German invasion was feared.

In addition to our games, we listened for the legendary bells of the lost village church somewhere under the sea and also searched for treasure in the muddy runnels between the ancient tree stumps exposed at very low tides, only returning home at meal and bed times. This was a completely free childhood where imagination, largely uninfluenced by adults or clouded by the complexities of modern society, could roam free and even run riot. Sadly, it was one which most modern children can no longer enjoy.

Looking back, we remember the best and worst of times, with the remainder fading into the background. The former were of bright summer mornings on the beach with our bodies luxuriating in warm sunshine. On one side, blue water reflected myriad flashing stars from a sun climbing up into the heaven and, on the other, gentle breezes stirred the marram grass on empty sand dunes. In between the sandy pebbly beach appeared as a broad golden highway leading to unknown distant delights. Here, I first learnt something about freedom, that often elusive concept which fires the imagination of all mankind.

The worst times came with bad weather when our East Coast seaside became a sombre inhospitable place, especially during winter, when cold winds, blowing in from across the North Sea, chilled us to the bone.

However, this was the place where I first recognised the ebbing and flowing of tides, the endless moods of the sky, the waxing and waning of seasons and the daily progress of the sun across the sky from the sea in the east to the distant hills in the west. Here, the seeds of my lifelong love of the great outdoors were sown.

The eyes of those who live on low lying flat ground have a natural affinity for higher places. In addition to providing natural focal points, these also mark out places of refuge, sometimes from human enemies, but at Chapel the adversary was almost always the sea, which had invaded the land many times in the past and could be expected to do so again in the future.

Although the village had its own tangible high ground in the form of the Sand Hills, there was also an ethereal one in the minds of many inhabitants. When I was young there was a persistent tale of mountains having once appeared in the sky above the sea. On childishly suggesting to my parents that these might have been a bank of cloud, I was told that this was not so because houses and trees had been clearly visible upon them. Having at that time never seen a hill of respectable size, my imagination ran riot and a picture of great heights with houses and trees scattered all over them became fixed in my mind. Years later, on discovering the reality of Northern Europe's wild bare mountain tops, they immediately hooked me for life, but provided no answer to the old puzzle. I suppose it was just possible that a mirage of a populated part of the Norwegian coast might once have appeared in the sky above the sea.

In spite of the great personal freedom, I later realised that our seemingly adventurous expeditions had only taken us northwards along the beach to Anderby Creek, southwards for one and a half miles towards Skegness and inland along quiet country roads to the village of Hogsthorpe.

Children did not often leave the village in those days and then it was mostly by bus to Skegness, our nearest local town. Occasionally, our family also travelled on from there by train to visit our grandparents in Boston and Spalding.

The young have no concept of tawdriness so, for me, Skegness was a glittering exotic place. Among its many spendours there were two features of lasting intense personal interest in the form of imitation rock faces and archways beside the boating lake on the sea front. Never having seen any genuine rocks, I could not take my eyes off them. They had a forgotten Germanic name and presumably the designer had intended to introduce a piece of far off mountainous Switzerland into the very flat Skegness holiday scene. However, he would never have imagined the profound impression it was to make on a local boy. Although not recognised as such at the time, this was the first manifestation of my future love for rugged places.

In 1938 my mother took my three year old sister Heather and I on a unique holiday to our Aunty Madge's family home at Lewes in Sussex. This, my first expedition into the wider reaches of England, was not to be repeated for another eight years. The journey was almost as exciting as the holiday itself. While crossing central London by taxi, the crowds of people, the busy traffic, the big buildings and the wide streets all proved awesome, especially as my concept of the capital as the earth's largest city, and centre of the greatest Empire which the world had ever known, had been formed at a small patriotic school in a remote corner of England.

Even this striking encounter could not compare with my first sight of the South Downs from the electric train as it crossed the Weald. None of my preconceptions were like the reality of this long rolling green ridge standing high above the surrounding countryside. In my excitement I could not wait to get onto them. Fortunately, the family were keen walkers so it was not long before we were exploring the tops of Offham Hill, Mount Harry and Black Cap and the long deep combes which nestled into their dip

18

slopes. Here was a wide open countryside without fences and hedges where people could wander at will and I revelled in the new freedom. In addition, there were exciting walks along the rolling tops of the dazzling white cliffs where the Downs met the sea. By the time we returned home this eight year old had made an important career decision. I was now determined to work hard and get on in the world so that upon growing up I could come and live in this lovely area.

On board the train heading back north from Kings Cross, many passengers were soldiers and sailors in uniform. Whether or not this was normal at the time I do not know, but later I wondered whether it might have been a portent for the future.

There is another memory of that journey. From Grantham, a winding journey with stops at every isolated country station took us back to Skegness. It was a lovely warm high summer day and everywhere the harvest was being gathered in by horse-drawn reapers and their numerous human helpers. Country children mostly spent their summer holidays at home and every time the train came to a halt, little crowds of them stood beside the track to wave at us through the clouds of steam and smoke issuing from the engine.

CHAPTER TWO

BANISHMENT

The young life idyll ended much sooner than it might have done. During my early years war was always an unpleasant entity lurking in the background, apparent from the older generation's obvious distress about the Great War, the sight of my father's wounds and those of badly maimed ex-soldiers who were still struggling on and dying around us. Now, there was serious talk of another war with the Germans, or 'the Jerries', as they were then universally known and it began a year later in September 1939.

My father's small architectural business, based on holiday coast developments, collapsed overnight. For a time he became a part-time member of the Observer Corps, but this income was insufficient to support the family. Then, in early summer 1940, our home at Chapel was packed up, Dad went away to do war work in the Midlands and my mother, sister and I moved south to her former home town of Spalding, where other members of her family still lived.

Life in the village had now become unpleasant, with air raids by both night and day. Our former wide playground was now banned to us, the new occupants being poorly clad and ill-equipped escapees from Dunkirk, who hastily dug trenches and erected barbed wire entanglements to deter a possible German seaborne invasion. Although I looked forward to the change at the time, there were soon to be sad longings for my former friends, the sea, the beach and the Sand Hills.

Before moving on I will say a few words about Chapel St. Leonards. Although the village which I knew in the 1930's was already changing, it would still have been recognisable to earlier generations of my family who had lived there. Since then there have been vast changes, wrought by a combination of both nature and man. Alas, the lovely Sand Hills have all gone, destroyed in a series of storms, especially the notorious death-dealing sea surge of 1953, and these have been replaced by a stark concrete sea wall. Gone, too, are the former meadows and small family farms of my youth, with the land now submerged beneath a dense carpet of bungalows and caravans.

My next eight years were spent in Spalding and, during that time, there were few walks apart from one that was to have an important bearing on later developments.

Perhaps Spalding was never as bad as I came to regard it. It had a large church, the remains of a medieval priory and a current population of around fifteen thousand. However, I experienced the town at its worst, for those were the bleak war years when money was tight, food short and every shop all but empty. The one major air raid in 1941 caused few deaths, but left many town centre buildings and shops either totally destroyed or badly damaged, and these remained largely unrepaired until after the war had ended.

However, Spalding was surrounded by vast low-lying Fens and it was these which I hated the most. Their monotonous man-made flatness was composed of straightened rivers, straight drains, straight drainage ditches, straight banks and straight roads. In addition, the paucity of trees, hedges and grass left few places where wild flowers could grow. During those critical wartime years, every square yard of land was under intense cultivation because the nation faced starvation as a result of successful German U-Boat attacks on the Atlantic convoys. But for me, with a yearning to explore new wilder countrysides, these surroundings came to represent a vast prison.

Within this vast disagreable scene, the lowest fens, which had only succumbed to drainage a hundred or so years before, proved to be the worst. These wide empty spaces had a sullen character, as though impatiently waiting for the time when they could revert once more to watery wastes full of fish and wildfowl. If recent rising sea level predictions are correct, then this change, unimaginable when I was a boy, could now come about. During our spare time my cousins and I at first walked along local country roads to a solitary poplar tree, at a junction which we named Lone Star, in deference to the cowboy and indian stories and films which we loved.

Today's Fens, in spite of the same dreary levels, are rather different from the scene which I knew in the 1940's. Firstly, many trees and bushes now break up the former empty vistas and, secondly, the small sleepy villages, once the homes of land workers, have become extensive modern urban settlements and, as a result, much of the former empty isolated character of the Fens has now gone.

Although Spalding was surrounded by fens, distant hills were to be seen along part of the western skyline. This higher ground was clearly very different from the immediate surroundings because rolling slopes, hedges, trees and woods were all visible on fine days. I often looked at these hills as a potential place of escape. Although a cliche, on one occasion I gazed at this upland over a field of ripening wheat waving gently in the breeze and imagined it to be a magic island on the other side of a golden sea. Yet I was by no means alone in holding these deferential views because this higher ground was known locally as the Highlands. Althought similar to the Wolds at a distance, I was later to learn that they were composed of limestone.

At my instigation on a damp dull day, my cousins and I, wearing our school clothes and navy gabardine macintoshes, set out on foot towards the small town of Bourne, with the object of reaching these hills. At first, we made good progress along a succession of straight sections of main road, but on arriving at Guthram Gowt, approximately halfway there, it became clear that we would not be able to reach our goal. By now, the tempting charms of these hills were clearly visible in much greater detail than before, but proper acquaintance would have to wait for some future date.

Motor traffic on country roads was very light during the war years. When a solitary car came along the driver unexpectedly stopped and then gently questioned us about who we were and what we were doing. It soon transpired that this was a business associate of my uncle and he then went on to ask us if we would like a lift back to the town, an offer which we could not refuse in our weary condition. If he ever said anything about this escapade to my uncle, I never heard of it. However, that failed exploit was the first of a lifetime's long walks which, in due course, would lead me through many wild and beautiful scenes.

CHAPTER THREE

BREAK OUT

Although relevant to later events, this chapter has little to do with walking. Few civilians left their homes during the war years because money was short, travel might increase exposure to enemy action, the wartime railway system was unreliable and, most important of all, the government actively discouraged the public from travelling.

However, I soon discovered that it was possible to provide my own means of escape from Spalding. During those troubled times everyone was encouraged to do their bit towards the war effort and for youngsters this meant land work during school holidays. Even the timing of our summer break was changed to coincide with the potato harvest. Although horses were being replaced by tractors, farming was still a labour intensive industry, with gangs hoeing weeds from growing crops and later in the season picking peas, potatoes and onions. I disliked the drudgery and boredom of this work, but although the pay was poor, equivalent to around three new pence per hour, after my first spell I was able to give my mother some upkeep money and purchase a second-hand bicycle.

This was a pre-war Raleigh Tourer with cable brakes and a Sturmey Archer three speed hub gear. Over the next six years this treasured machine carried me many hundreds of miles. Its three gears may have been adequate for the modest hills encountered along the way, but the wind always mattered most, being either an enemy or a friend and rarely anything in-between. Blowing unimpeded across the flat empty spaces of the Fens, it led to long slow slogs when in front, and speedy almost effortless cruising when behind, an effect increased when we were obliged to wear our old-fashioned oilcloth cycle capes as protection from rain.

In those all but traffic free days, the expression 'the song of the open road' still had true meaning. Sun, rain, wind and occasional calm were our only companions and fresh air and big skies all that we met along the way. By this means I now rediscovered the freedom once enjoyed on Chapel beach. My companions were my cousins in early days and my school pal Norman on later ones, but sometimes I also roamed alone. In retrospect these long excursions to remote places now seem foolhardy. We had little money in our pockets and if mishaps had occurred there were no means of communicating with our families or of them helping us. But such is the blind confidence of the young that our enjoyment never included consideration of possible problems.

Predictably, my first trip took me to the long sought after Highlands and it proved an unforgettable experience. Until that sunny day I had only seen the muddy tidal waters of the Rivers Welland and Witham slithering forwards and backwards with the tide or the seeming stagnant waters of the numerous drains and dykes of the region. Now, at Kate's Bridge, just where the River Glen finally left the uplands for the Fens, I saw dancing sunlit ripples of the crystal clear water on its downward flow. For a long time I stood transfixed. It is doubtful whether any first-time visitor to Niagara Falls could have been more entranced.

A return visit to the sea of my early childhood was now a high priority. From maps Spalding did not seem to be far from the coast but, as I was soon to discover to my great disappointment, hereabouts the end of the land did not necessarily correspond with the beginning of the sea. Until now I had only been familiar with the very sharp boundary between the two at Chapel St. Leonards and the white cliffs where the South Downs met the sea. So, on first topping the final sea bank near Holbeach St. Matthew, eager anticipation was suddenly replaced by utter dismay. Ahead lay the vast dark sea marsh of the Wash with only a glimmer of water in the far north. Defeated, my cousins and I returned home, but we were resolved to try again at another place.

Next time we approached the coast near Gedney Drove End where a nearby channel led to the River Nene. Memories of that day are crystal clear. The sun was shining and the top of the sea wall presented us, as before, with a greenish-brown marsh, but now this led to shining yellow sands and on to a distant blue sea. The opportunity was far too good to miss. Leaving our bikes and footgear on the bank, we headed out into the marsh, intent on reaching the sands. The seeming dead level marsh soon proved to be otherwise because its flat surface was riven by deep, twisting and very muddy creeks. These were almost dry at the current low tide and did not impede our progress overmuch. However, long before we reached the golden sands, the muddy water changed direction and began slurping back up the creeks at an alarming speed.

Aware of the danger, we turned and hastened back. But our progress could not match that of the flood now swirling into the maze of creeks between us and the safety of the sea bank. Repeated clamberings down, across and up increasingly wet creeks slowed our progress, but fortunately the visibility that day was good. As the tide gathered pace, each creek crossing became increasingly difficult. Finally, we just managed to reach the sea bank before the muddy water topped our legs. By now exhausted, we collapsed onto the grassy bank top. Our escape had been a close run thing because we could not swim at the time and there would have been no help at that lonely place as wartime regulations forbade public presence. In retrospect, I believe that it was the striking similarity between my youthful sea marsh creeks and the grough sundered peat moors of adult life that made the latter all the more attractive and familiar to me when I first came upon them.

After that sobering experience, my enthusiasm to reach the sea waned until a large scale map of the Wash gave me the idea for a new attempt. A feature known as the Scalp had now caught my eye. This consisted of two parallel banks on each side of the Boston shipping channel as it left the land behind and headed out into the Wash. I reasoned that this was the only place where the sea could be reached from South Lincolnshire.

The northernmost of these two banks, necessitating a detour through Boston, seemed to be the best access point. Norman and I reached our destination on a fine summer day to find that, for once, our luck was in. The sea was not only lapping both sides of the bank on which we stood, but also stretched away to the right, front and left. Success had come at last and what a joy it was! Norman may have lacked my absolute passion for the sea, because he had not lived and slept with it for the first ten years of his life, but on this occasion my enthusiasm infected him. This scene was not all, within a short space of time the growing sound of diesel engines attracted our attention. Louder and louder it grew, reaching a crescendo as six military landing craft in line astern under the command of a Royal Navy lieutenant came round the bend in the river. They passed us by and then headed out to sea, turning north and away. We watched them until out of sight and by then the tide was visibly ebbing.

The Highlands lived up to their long held promise. These belonged to very different Englands from the ones which I had known at Chapel St. Leonards and Spalding. Previously only viewed in picture books, I now had the opportunity to fall in love with their reality. The ups and downs of the roads, hardly ever severe, led past hedgerows and trees bordering arable fields and meadows before entering successions of spinneys and woods. Dips in the roads crossed tiny fast flowing becks to reach small old villages with stone dwellings topped by stone, red tiled or thatched roofs. Nowadays, I would describe these villages as Cotswold look-alikes, but that description is not one that I would have understood at the time. The Jurassic Limestone Ridge heads north eastwards from Dorset along the Cotswold Ridge before extending across Middle England and up the length of Lincolnshire. All the way along its length there are similar golden brown stone buildings.

Although choice is difficult, my favourite Highland village was probably Castle Bytham. From the top of a slope, it overlooked the massive earthworks of its former Norman castle. In their turn, the thatched and multicoloured tiled roofs of the dwellings were crowned by an attractive Norman church. This was a favourite stopping place for both its beauty and pervasive peace. In those days the village had a railway and station and after leaving home I sometimes travelled this way. When the train drew in and stopped, all the world suddenly became very still apart from a gentle hiss of steam and only rarely did a passenger get on or off.

The prime place in these new-found lands was Stamford, a mellow golden old town full of striking architecture. Although of a similar size to Spalding, located on the same river and only twenty miles away, the difference between the two was so profound that they could have been a thousand miles apart. While full of admiration for Stamford, at that time I was completely unaware that I had accidentally stumbled on one of the most beautiful towns in the land. On many occasions I came riding this way and never grew tired of it.

There was also a very different River Welland at Stamford. No longer tidal, its clear waters flowed past low hills on the upstream side of the town where Roman Ermine Street had once forded the water. Well aware that Roman legions had once passed this way, for me in those heady days it seemed as though I had at last arrived at the heart of England and English history.

Peace brought an end to air raids and most of the fighting and killing, but food rationing remained severe and improvements to our austere lifestyle were slow in coming. At least people had begun to move around once more. In 1946 my sister, mother and I returned to Lewes. The lovely Downs, apart from wartime intrusions such as the huge radar masts along the coast, which until recently had given warning of approaching enemy aircraft, were just as I remembered them and my long-held wish to eventually come and live in this area remained. Although previously unrecognised by an eight year old, I now realised that part of the attraction of the South Downs lay in their feminine curves and valleys. Although the extent of our walking was only moderate, one exhilarating ramble with my uncle and cousin took us over the Downs above Kingston to a view of the distant Isle of Wight before passing through the pretty little hamlet of Telscombe and on to the white cliffs at Peacehaven.

The summer of 1947 was truly memorable. With the possible exception of 1976 it was the longest and hottest summer that I have ever known. As the British Empire disintegrated with increasing rapidity, Norman and I lost interest in the outside world while playing tennis, practising cricket, swimming in the Fenland drains and flirting shyly with the girls from the nearby High School. We also cycled from Spalding down to Lewes, staying at Youth Hostels at Cambridge and Rochford along the way. That journey, for the most part along nearly deserted roads, passed through several different regions of England, most of them new to me. I fell in love with each in turn, especially the one on the last day when we cycled up and down across the Weald to Lewes. Incidentally, during that journey, we were sustained by tinned iron rations which had originally been prepared for the armed forces but were now on sale at Youth Hostels.

From these experiences I had discovered that the bicycles of the day could not take me to the newly discovered wild and remote places that I now wished to explore. In any event my life was now about to undergo a radical change.

CHAPTER FOUR

MOVING ON

The opportunity to go to Imperial College in London in the autumn of 1948 was welcome because I would learn more about subjects which interested me, my National Service would be deferred, there would be the opportunity to meet other contemporaries and I would also be close to the part of England which I had come to love.

However, the first year was not a happy one. The only accommodation available near the College was a lodging house where the food was inferior and the other inhabitants foreign, mostly from the Indian Sub Continent. In addition, the majority of my fellow students were wartime ex-sevicemen who had little time for the few 'schoolboys' in their midst. Apart from myself and one other, this small minority were locals with established home lives in the outer suburbs. In these circumstances it is not surprising that I failed to meet any kindred spirits at this time.

For a time London, with its famous buildings, fine monuments, wide roads, busy traffic and novel underground system, proved fascinating for a country boy. At weekends I systematically explored all the famous places, before concentrating on museums for their fascinating contents, free entry and warm interiors. However, the appalling wartime bomb damage still remained largely unrepaired and the capital city was also unrelentlessly drab, dirty and very run down. The perpetually filthy atmosphere finally contributed to the breakdown of my health with bronchitis.

Now longing for open countryside, my attention switched to the large inner parks and later I went further afield to the likes of Richmond, Kew and Greenwich. But even here the air was never free from London's tainted atmosphere.

By the end of that first year, I was determined that my future walks would be in the countryside and, hopefully, in the company of like-minded contemporaries. This objective required a change in lifestyle which was made partly by myself and also, unconsciously, by my parents.

The second year at college was altogether better. With no hope of gaining a place in the extremely limited space of the college's one small hall of residence, I moved out into the suburbs and lodged with a family in South Wimbledon during term-time for the next two years. Wimbledon was a good choice because it was on the District Line to the college and also an important junction for Southern Region rail services.

Years before, circumstances had thwarted my wish to become a countryside walker and instead I took up cycling. Now the time had come to make the change. In the current circumstances it took some time to find like minded contemporaries, but when I did they could not have been better. By coincidence their original base at Wimbledon Technical College was close to my term-time home, but by then its members, of both sexes in their twenties and ranging from medical students to electricians, came from far and wide across London. The group gelled well, united by shared interests and enjoyment. Fortunately some core members were familiar with the country footpath system to the south of the capital and with them I made my first proper rambles in all weathers, occasionally finishing in the dark on short winter days. The extensive

Southern Electric rail network provided a wide choice of starting points and at least on one occasion we travelled to the South Downs. With no market for walking gear at the time, all of us went out in our well worn everyday clothes.

Rare encounters with other walkers were occasions for cheerful greetings. We also met flocks of cyclists along roads which, unlike rambling, had remained a popular pastime after the war and we sometimes made good use of their surviving wooden-hutted cafes. The comradeship of this walking group after my lone urban wanderings of the previous year came to mean a great deal to me.

My affection for the Weald was now reinforced. This rolling countryside, with paddocks, hedges, trees and extensive woods, provided seemingly endless attractive scenes, ranging from surprisingly pretty villages, complete with delightful small churches and wood-clad homes, to massed trees comparable to those of prehistoric times. Fifteen hundred years after the Saxons had recognised the region as the Weald (Wald), its name was still appropriate. However, it was some time before I recognised that many of these pretty villages, some still retaining their attractive hammer ponds, had once been at the centre of England's iron-making industry before coal replaced wood in its manufacture and the industry had moved away. At first I found it hard to credit that these same surroundings had once been notable for ravaged woodland, smoke and grime. With this realisation there came an early comforting reassurance that former human exploitation of a scene can sometimes provide the basis for its latter day beauty.

My parents' unconscious contribution to my reorganised lifestyle was their purchase of a house in Nottingham, a lively and fascinating city compared to lonely Spalding now that all my friends had left the town. In addition, it was close to the upland areas of England which I was now keen to explore.

I still did some cycling and predictably my early trips headed towards this higher country. The first part of the route crossed what was then the biggest coalfield in the land. The mines and the industries which followed them had been imposed on agricultural land and former villages had become nondescript towns. Now the pits have all gone, their only apparent legacy being a few surviving miners' cottages and oddly shaped hills created from old spoil tips following contouring and replanting, just a few of the many changes since I first encountered an area then still recognisable as the setting for D. H. Lawrence's early novels.

Beyond the coalfield, the hills grew in size and at Ambergate I entered the tree covered high-sided valley of the River Derwent. There, at the relatively late age of nineteen, I finally entered Upland England. A nearby large mill, originally water powered, filled the valley bottom. Then the sides closed in until the river was flowing through a gorge, with the massive white limestone cliffs of High Tor on the right and the taller gritstone Heights of Abraham on the left, scenes that I had been wanting to explore for some time. Aware that this was only the edge of the Peak District, I now wished to discover all that it had to offer.

Frustrated by lack of information on where one could walk in unfamiliar countryside, a problem currently exacerbated by the dilapidated state of many footpaths, I knew that it was necessary to find a walking group in Nottingham if the Peak District was to be enjoyed to the full. Again the task was not easy, but I eventually came across the Curlew Rambling Club and this was the start of a happy relationship which was to continue for the next three years.

The Curlews were a small all-male walking group who considered themselves to be the hard men of

Nottingham's walking community, a claim not overly impressive because the number of active walkers in the area was then minuscule. The members' ages ranged from the mid-twenties to, in the case of one individual, the sixties. At first I thought Bill far too old for long energetic walks, but that was before I came to know his abilities! The transport manager for a firm of dyers in Nottingham, he not only loved walking but also seemed totally at ease with life. The only time I ever saw him disconcerted was when a planned lunch time stop proved to be a pub with only a six-day licence. The other leading members were Alan, a lively lad with a ready quip for every occasion who worked for a firm of furniture manufacturers in Nottingham, and Peter, a quiet, organised, reserved and rather deaf young man, who had been an army corporal and was now a member of the office staff at Ericssons in Beeston.

Due to their more challenging walking area, the club members were better equipped than my Surrey friends. With no walking equipment on the market, they mostly wore ex-WD gear which was currently plentiful and cheap. This clothing was generally well made apart from the rubberised ground sheets which were both heavy and provided little protection from the weather. When Peter appeared wearing the first purpose-made walking cape that any of us had ever seen he created considerable interest.

Robust boots were essential for all-weather Peakland walking, but only army surpluses were currently available. Although reasonably durable, their soles were no match for rough rocky ground, so we hammered the currently popular triple headed tricounis into them. These additions successfully prevented excessive wear, but proved very noisy when walking along streets and dangerously slippery on all iron surfaces and even on White Peak limestone after it became polished by wear and wetted by rain. I first encountered boots with rubberised soles in 1954 and these had been made for the Commandos. All of us carried ex-army haversacks or rucksacks which were well made but far from ideal for our purposes. Again Peter was the only exception with his treasured pre-war Bergen model.

Uncharacteristically, as it later turned out, I first joined the Curlews on a ramble through the gentle countryside to the south of Nottingham. My memories of that day include the warm welcome they gave me and also the surprisingly lovely rendition of the popular ballad 'If I were a blackbird....' which the patrons of a village inn were rendering when we called in for a lunchtime drink. From that time onwards, whenever possible, I joined them on their rambles.

The Curlews' walking country of choice was to the north and west of Matlock, but not in the vicinity of that small town. This included the gritstone edges leading up to the high moors together with much of the limestone country. Even in those uncrowded days I got the distinct impression that the club members regarded Matlock as a little too touristy for their tastes. We often used the express Nottingham-Manchester bus service to Bakewell, Taddington or Buxton and from these places gained access to Longstone Edge, the long line of prominent gritstone edges backed by moors which overlook the upper Derwent Valley and the chain of dales leading up from Monsal Dale through Millers Dale to Chee Dale.

A rare excursion train took me to Edale for my initiation to the lovely lost world of Kinder Scout. Edale is a broad valley surrounded by hills whose names soon became old friends, Win Hill, Lose Hill, Back Tor, Mam Tor, Rushup Edge and, extending along the length of its northern side, the mighty Kinder Scout plateau. Although there were few hill walkers in those days, Edale station became busy for a short time after an excursion train arrived. The ramble that day was short, up Grindsbrook, across the plateau top, along Kinder River to the Downfall and finally a return over the highest point. The track across the meadow to Grindsbrook was then only wide enough for two to walk side by side, not the six or seven lane highway of more recent times. Kinder Scout has no summit. Steep bracken covered slopes climb up to weather beaten edges penetrated by rugged gullies where small streams tumble from the plateau. These edges, eroded into weird shapes, provide wide views in fair weather, but only a few yards back from the lip all is changed. Here, the intimate world of thick peat beds, riven by deep winding groughs at first reminded me of the muddy creeks in the Wash. This plateau defies description due to its extreme contrasts. For it is simultaneously clean and dirty, fascinating and repulsive and both stimulating and exhausting. It is clean because fresh winds of heaven blow across this high place, dirty with the treacherous deep peat mush, fascinating for its uniqueness, repulsive because it is a desert with minimal life and both exhausting and stimulating because in both rain and fine it always presents a challenge. The plateau ends as quickly as it began. Peat suddenly giving way to boulders and these soon lead to the rugged cliffs of the Downfall.

Kinder walkers were then males of two distinct types, a few hoary veterans of the Kinder Scout wars of the 1930s and a scattering of younger walkers like myself. By the early 1950s access to Kinder Scout had been won, but there was still lingering bitterness among the older men for the punishment, both physical and legal, that they had suffered. There were also tales, often at second or third hand, of current unpleasant confrontations with gamekeepers, but I never met with any here. Although I have since climbed many higher hills and mountains, for me, this grim wild wet desert plateau ringed by weathered gritstone outcrops, will always represent the nearest thing I know to the roof of the world.

Prominent memories of those Curlew rambles include a bitterly cold walk along an otherwise deserted Dove Dale covered in snow. Nowadays, this beautiful valley can become very crowded, but on that special occasion we had its unforgettable ruggedness all to ourselves. Sometimes only snapshot memories remain of those rambles. One is of sitting in the warm kitchen of a farmhouse high in the hills. After a strenuous walk through thick snow, we were glad to sit down on old wooden chairs with our steaming legs stretched out in front of an open fire. Meanwhile, the elderly couple of the house were preparing a large pot of tea. This was made from our collected tea leaf contributions brought from home in twists of paper. Now all but forgotten, the food rationing that came with the Second World War continued long after it had ended. At other times we called at the Curlew's favourite watering hole, the pub at Wardlow, where we could sit, sup and admire the young fresh beauty of the landlord's wife.

My first university summer break took me to Shell's Shellhaven Oil Refinery on the Essex shore of the Thames Estuary. Here, the surrounding semi-urban scene discouraged any form of rambling. However, the refinery site did have one redeeming feature in providing a grandstand view of passing ships. Of the many different types of vessel, the most beautiful by far were the flocks of cargo-carrying sailing barges which often tacked backwards and forwards across the estuary.

The following year, my vacation work was at the Power Gas Corporation in Stockton on Tees. On the way there by train, my eager anticipation of the North Yorkshire Moors was heightened by their pleasing dark outline along the eastern horizon. Of the two other students, one was Piet from Delft. He proved a kindred spirit, mostly, I think, because like me he had been brought up in flat countryside and therefore had a natural affinity for hills.

The summer weather was fine and every weekend we bussed to different walk starting points from Osmotherly overlooking the Vale of York in the west to Whitby on the coast in the east. Up here among the heather there was solitude and fresh air in abundance, contrasting with the smoky steelworks smudges to the north in the lower Tees Valley, which were periodically supplemented by bright orange-red plumes. To the south, the empty moors fell slowly away with only a hint of steep intervening valleys. At the time I was completely unaware that the rocks of this wild upland were similar to those of my tamed Highlands beside the Fens.

The prominent northern outlier known as Roseberry Topping became a favourite spot. It had been made more eye catching by an earlier collapse of one side of the hill due to iron ore mining. A monument to Captain Cook, a local man regarded as a great national hero during my village primary school days, also stood nearby. I did not climb this hill again until the late 1980s and that was in the company of some oil industry colleagues. Unfortunately, the mist that day was so thick that I saw nothing other than my companions all the way up to the top and back down again.

Even high up on these lonely moors there were obvious signs of former human activity. The combination of the iron ore found here, coal from nearby County Durham and limestone from the Pennines, came together to foster the development of Teeside's steel industry during the nineteenth century. These signs included old workings, a former railway and the remains of an incline which had once been used to lower laden ore wagons down to the valley below.

The dingy brown colour of North Yorkshire's massive cliffs did not detract from their impact. As the first high terrain encountered by north bound mariners, the region became known as Cliffland, which in due time was softened to Cleveland. Out on the coast, the true nature of the local climate became apparent, for although high summer and the weather fine, there was always a slight nip in the air.

After Teeside, Piet and I went our separate ways, but we kept in contact for a time through sporadic correspondence. Then, during a business trip to the Netherlands in the autumn of 1957, I called at his home in Delft and was surprised to find how much he had changed in demeanour if not in looks. The free happy spirit, who had wandered with me over the moors seven years before, was now a sober lecturer in engineering at Delft University and so was his wife who held a similar position at the same institution. On later reflection, I wondered whether he might have detected a like change in me.

My walking was curtailed during the first half of 1951 as final exams loomed. However, I did manage to spend three days with my London friends while they were on a youth hostelling tour around the northern Peak District. As they were not familiar with this part of the world, it fell to my lot to lead them over the challenging landscape of Kinder Scout. Down at the bottom, the weather had been cool and wet, but on reaching the tops a surprise lay in wait. Easter was early that year and the remains of thick snow from winter storms still filled the network of groughs on the plateau. There, the icy crusts often gave way up to knee level under our weight and this made progress very tiring and slow. This bleak hostile country was totally alien to my companions, more familiar with the tree bordered grassy paths of the South, and many soon showed signs of concern and exhaustion.

Up and down the groughs we struggled as I relied on my compass for direction when marauding sleet showers obliterated the view. An uncanny silence now prevailed in the failing light, apart from the piping voice of one participant, a pure social rambler always ever ready with banter. Fortunately, the gods were with us that day, but it was a very weary group whom I finally shepherded into the youth hostel at Rowland Cote. Needless to say, my relief at bringing my friends back to safety was great. Being wise after the event, I should not have tackled the route with an inexperienced party in these conditions. Yet, within an hour, all the participants had revived and after the evening meal they noisily recounted their individual Kinder Scout experiences to each other. Already I was beginning to detect some exaggerations and no doubt very tall stories were told in the London area during the following weeks.

Impromptu singing was popular at that time, but while Northern and Midland walkers usually rendered the likes of 'The Manchester Rambler', 'Jerusalem' or 'The Derby Rambling Club', my London friends concentrated on popular songs. Predictably after the Kinder excursion their favourite immediately became 'I traced her little footsteps through the snow.......'.

A distant echo of that event came back fifty years later. On retirement my wife and I moved to Exmoor where we soon met members of the local walking community. One of these was Andy, who had a similar passion for walking and we became good friends. Aware that he originally came from South London, once or twice I mentioned walking with a club in those parts around 1950 and 1951, There was no response. And I put this down to the fact that, because the local population was huge, it seemed rather unlikely that we would have met.

Then at a ramblers' lunch in 2001, around ten years

after our presumed first meeting, we got around to chatting about our former rambling experiences in the Weald and their striking similarity again made me wonder whether our paths could have crossed in those days. Looking for some helpful clues, I tried to remember the names of my companions at that time, but all that came to mind were those of two sisters.

'Did you ever come across Pam and Hilary Budd in those days?' I said.

The impact of this question was sudden and dramatic. Andy is not a person given to emotional display, but now he looked totally astonished and could only emit a series of incomprehensible noises. Finally a single word came out.

'Yes.'

I do not think that this disclosure was what is usually meant by "cherchez la femme", but a common link between our pasts was now revealed. I had taken Hilary out on a number of occasions and it transpired that he had been sweet on the same young lady at around the same time. Searching his memory, he remembered that there had been another shadowy person in her life called Brian who was a student from Nottingham. I, on the other hand, had no recollection of him whatsoever. But surely we must have met at some point. I looked at my few photos of the walking group and he was not on any of them. Simultaneously, Andy studied his own more comprehensive collection and one of them, taken at the top of Kinder Scout on that fateful Easter day in 1951, showed a shadowy unrecognisable figure standing behind the two sisters. Andy eventually identified it as me through a process of elimination and I recognised myself by the unusual American army cap which I wore at the time. On that long gone day the group was large, the challenge great. Memories had also faded and both of us had changed a good deal in the interim.

Shortly after this event my life moved on. All connections with London were severed when I became preoccupied with National Service and in the process I lost all contact with this rambling club and its members.

Although much of my future life remained uncertain in the summer of 1951, my leisure activity was now cast in bronze. Cycling days had finally been left behind and all that I now wanted was to wander along paths and tracks through quiet countrysides and over high wild hills. The fact that my chosen form of pleasure might have been regarded as cranky by society at large was no longer of any import.

CHAPTER FIVE

TO ENGLAND'S EXTREMES

With National Service looming, it seemed a good idea to pack in as much walking as possible during the summer of 1951. While waiting for call up I took a temporary job at the New Basford Gas Works in Nottingham to finance these trips.

When my friend Bill of the Curlews suggested that I could take a lift in one of his lorries which made a weekly trip to a hosiery works in Kendal, I leapt at the offer. We arrived at Kendal in the early afternoon and, after a perfunctory look at rows of clacking machines knitting woollen socks and confirming our arrangements for meeting again in a week's time, I caught an Ambleside bus.

Small rugged hills appeared ahead, a foretaste of the region that I was now about to enter. On topping a rise in the road, a splendid sunlit panorama of distant high peaks appeared above nearby Lake Windermere. Although my expectations were high, the scene was far more beautiful than I had ever imagined.

Leaving the bus at Troutbeck Bridge, I made my way up the valley towards the village of Troutbeck and its youth hostel. Rocky heights, the likes of which I had never seen or even dreamt of before, blocked the way ahead, engendering awe as well as admiration. Doubts about an absolute novice tackling these hills alone were reinforced by my very basic map which depicted few of these rocky features. On this first occasion, the mountains presented a confusing jumble, but by a year and a half later their individual shapes, names and the ways up and down them had become blazed on my mind. On that first evening I met three fellow hostellers from Liverpool of my own age. Two were old hands with the Lakes and they kindly let me tag along with them. I have long forgotten their names, but one was notable for his baggy ex-Royal Navy tropical white shorts. In a pristine condition when we first met, they soon acquired dirty marks and by the end of our time together had become a uniform grey.

Next morning we set out for Patterdale over Stoney Cove Pike. The previous day's fine weather had been replaced by humid very wetting Lake District summer rain which was to continue on and off for the remainder of that week. But this could not dampen my joy on being among these hills for the first time. We spent the next two nights at Patterdale, following the sharp arrete of Striding Edge up to Helvellyn on the day between. Photos studied earlier had not prepared me for the airiness of this high place.

Regrettably, my memories have become jumbled with the passage of time. On this first visit I recall walking over Fairfield Mountain in a downpour and then dropping down to Grasmere, but after that my recollection is blank until we reached Buttermere. From there we tackled Red Pike in fine weather and this was followed by a ridge walk over High Stile and High Crag down to the Scarth Gap Pass and the Black Sail Hut. This small single storey hostel, formerly a shepherd's hut, stands in the upper reaches of beautiful lonely Ennerdale which was to become my most loved Lakeland valley.

The downpour of late afternoon continued into evening. For a time there were no views because low cloud enveloped our world. After the evening meal the pleasant peaceful atmosphere of the place was disrupted by two unprepossessing Londoners. Nominally talking to each other, but in loud voices intending to impress the company at large, they held forth on their knowledge of the female anatomy and of their great successes with both young and mature members of the opposite sex. Bored by this distasteful display of distinctly dubious veracity, and feeling trapped within the narrow confines of the hut, I escaped outside into the fading light. The rain had ceased and gaps in the mist had opened up to reveal glimpses of lower hillsides across the valley. Here in total quiet, apart from rainwater still dripping steadily from the roof, I found I was not alone. A quiet North Country hosteler wearing an old fashioned flat cap was puffing away on a pipe. To me at the time he seemed old but was probably only middle aged. He nodded back at the door and muttered something about a bit of peace. After that nothing more was said as we both watched a line of slow moving light grey cloud moving along the dark sides of Pillar and Kirk Fell until the scene faded away with the light from the sky.

On the following day we passed deep bleak Wastwater, with its huge tumbling screes, to arrive at Wasdale Youth Hostel and on the next continued over the hills to the upper Duddon Valley. Having said goodbye to my friends of the past few days, I set out for Ambleside and my return journey. Time was pressing and I followed the tarmac lane over Wrynose Pass, a most enjoyable experience in those traffic free days. As Windermere's long silver water, marking the southern boundary of the Lake District, came into view, I wondered when I would next be here. With National Service ahead the interval could have been long, but circumstance's were to prove otherwise.

The Lake District has been likened to a wheel with mountain ridges as its spokes. During that first week we crossed these spokes close to the hub marked by shapely

Great Gable. I had also discovered that this small region contains such a large number of rugged mountains, hills, becks, rivers, lakes and tarns that it would take a very long time to explore them all.

So at the relatively late age of twenty-one, I had at last encountered real mountains. Although I have since climbed many higher ones, often far afield, none have ever matched the wide scenic variety of the Lakeland hills which ranges from wild rugged tops down to lovely lakes and valleys with their homely settlements. Distance and close proximity each had their own beauty, and during that summer trip I was particularly struck by the profusion of wild flowers growing in the natural rockeries at one's feet. After a week in this paradise I was now about to return to the gasworks.

My old school chum Norman and I had been apart for more than two years, but in the summer of 1951 we eventually came together again for a visit to the Festival of Britain, and that autumn also took a walking-cum-hitch-hiking holiday to the South West. Nowadays I know rather more about our Lands End trip than my earlier one to the Lakes because I wrote a journal which has survived.

We travelled from Nottingham to Taunton by a combination of bus journeys and hitch-hikes. Disparate observations along the way included the objectionable sight of Teddy Boys with their hair in pronounced quiffs and wearing huge-shouldered jackets, bright waistcoats and yellow socks. These specimens were lounging around in a milk bar close to Worcester's venerable cathedral. Then came the pleasing distant view of the miniature Malvern mountains which was followed after nightfall by ocean-going ships moored alongside the city centre in Bristol, a scene which I likened to the Golden Horn at Istanbul! I may have recently been re-reading Kinglake's 'Eothen', a perrenial favourite.

Walking began at the tiny hamlet of Triscombe below the Quantocks. Fresh air carried on a slight breeze provided a tonic after the diesel smells and exhaust fumes of the preceding day. We prepared our first holiday meal on an old fashioned tinplate methylated spirit cooker in a sheltered spot near the hill top.

Here was another part of Upland Britain. The long Quantock ridge extended towards the Bristol Channel and we followed a lonely track along the top surrounded by heather and gorse still in full bloom. Wide distant views included the green Somerset Levels, the Mendips, the waters of Bridgwater Bay and the hills of Exmoor. In addition, the now broad Bristol Channel was also backed by the coast, hills and mountains of Wales. In my ignorance I first mistook Steep Holm, an island of pincushion shape in the middle of the Channel, for the more famous Lundy, but in reality that lies further to the west where the Bristol Channel merges into the open Atlantic.

The sky above Exmoor's hills was already grey. Then our immediate sunshine failed, followed by ominous gusts of wind which rattled the dry leaves of trees on descent to the youth hostel at Holford. Later, a disagreeable combination of loud snoring room mates, lashing rain and a howling wind led to a disturbed night.

The new day had a strong wind, but the rain had gone and the sun shone intermittently from gaps in white fluffy clouds. Dunster's fairy tale castle appeared like an illustration from a child's story book come to life. Years later I was to discover that this building was more of a Victorian confection than a medieval stronghold. Dunster appeared little changed from medieval times, but we did not dally here because famed Selworthy was already in our sights.

The climb above the little town was hard going, but

the surrounding trees, their leaves just turning brown and gold, provided shelter. Once out on the open top all hell was let loose. Here, the wind was venomous, spinning both of us round and knocking us off our feet. Breathing became almost impossible when facing into the wind. With youthful determination we progressed in a long series of zigzags in between the strongest gusts. After a seemingly interminable time we finally crawled into the shelter of a boundary bank where the hill top tree plantations began. There we were obliged to rest for a considerable time before continuing on our way. Since then no high winds have ever quite matched the one on that day. Years later, much to my wry amusement, I discovered that the open top where we had fought our long battle with the wind was none other than the 'purple headed mountain' of the joyful hymn 'All Things Bright and Beautiful'!

As the wind went away, the heavy rain came. Although soaked we continued on through the trees to Selworthy. With our clammy wet clothing and the sight of dreary rain streaked thatched cottages with their sad drooping flowers, the reputed prettiest village in England held little appeal. However, we did enjoy several very refreshing cups of hot tea while there. We spent that night in Minehead Youth Hostel, in those days an impressive but rather gloomy mansion above the town centre, which has long since been demolished.

I walked on to Lynmouth, but Norman, still suffering from the preceding day's battering, took the bus. He had had a form of rheumatic fever during his National Service days which weakened his stamina and may also have been a factor in his premature death in middle age. Ironically, our school day circumstances were now reversed. Then he had been a strong healthy farm boy while I was a weakling town dweller prone to bilious attacks and bouts of bronchitis.

The new morning was fine and sunny. Leaving the old thatched and yellow washed cottages of upper Minehead behind, I headed away through trees to high coastal moorland above the sea. Lovely views across the Channel were disturbed by one small smudge of grey smoke on the Welsh coast. This marked the new Margam steelworks, then regarded as a symbol of Britain's new post war industrial revival and a precursor of the golden age which everyone assumed to be just around the corner. On approaching Selworthy Beacon, the riot of purple heather and golden gorse became badly churned up, a relic left by army tanks during the recent war years. Then I doubted whether nature could reclaim it, but time has shown that there was no need for concern.

The ground in front opened up to reveal the Vale of Porlock, and there I encountered the first humans since leaving Minehead. After lunch in a cafe in Porlock with only two Salvation Army women for company, I looked in on the deserted old Ship Inn at Porlock Weir, until recent times the haunt of seafarers.

Lynmouth was still distant and time was becoming short. Beyond there was Culbone, a hamlet consisting of an ancient small church and two dwellings, where for sixpence I bought a pot of tea, drinking five cups in quick succession before hurrying on. Then all signs of a path continuing along the coast were lost and to avoid wasting time seeking something that might not exist, I headed inland to follow the main coast road to Lynmouth. The afternoon was now cool and cloudy. The road, a thin ribbon of tarmac bounded by strips of close cropped grass, headed across open undulating heather moor rolling away in gentle curves up to the far southern horizon. The holiday season was over and only occasional traffic disturbed the peace. With passing time the wind rose and my tiredness grew as the same road and moorland seemed about to continue on forever. Then the top of Countisbury's grey church tower came into view and on discovering that a bus was about to leave for Lynmouth, I jumped on board. From there it only took a few minutes to reach the seaside.

Many years elapsed before I again came this way and then the absence of the extensive moorland which I had once tramped across at first seemed like a perverse trick of the mind. Then I noticed that the poor meadows of this area were bounded by rusty wire fencing with stained concrete posts, and not traditional Exmoor earth bank boundaries faced by stone. In a flash it was clear that the lovely heather moorland had sadly been lost, in what I felt to be ironic circumstances because the region became a National Park shortly after my first visit.

Lynmouth provided a reminder of the Lake District which I had first explored a few months before. Both had precipitous wooded and rocky hillsides above rushing streams and even the architecture was similar. The latter was explained by the fact that both areas had developed into tourist resorts at the beginning of the nineteenth century. However, the one striking difference was that the lakes had been replaced here by huge hills falling into the broad Bristol Channel. The geological histories of both regions also had some parallels because the old worn-down hills and mountains of both had been extensively modified around the time of the Ice Ages. Here a high fast flowing river had broken through its valley wall, initially as a tall waterfall tumbling into the sea, before cutting a deep winding valley back into the hills.

Sounds and sight were not encouraging on the following morning. Outside the bedroom window the river was a swirling lashing brown flood bounding over the large boulders and a howling wind was peppering everything with large raindrops. With foresight I might have regarded this scene as ominous, but at the time it was only fascinating. A year later Lynmouth's infamous flood disaster cost thirty-five people their lives and changed the village forever. I have since failed to identify the B&B establishment where we stayed and it may have been one of the buildings which was washed away.

After breakfast we set out up the East Lyn Valley. Although the clouds were lifting, dank mist pockets still clung to the waterside. At Watersmeet we enjoyed a pot of tea at the cafe, which was empty apart from two other young men of similar age. Over a daily newspaper the four of us talked about the current troubles in the Middle East, moving on to National Service and whether we might soon find ourselves involved in a major war again. After a meal in an upstream glade beside the water, Norman and I talked about the supposed exploits of the local Doone family and, reminded by our present surroundings, this led on to reminiscences about the cowboy and indian films which we had once loved.

Beyond the valley a new cool wind from the sea was blowing over the Foreland. There we foolishly took a very narrow path across a steep hillside above cliffs and sea. By then the wind had become strong and a single false step could have led to disaster.

Next day we soon reached the magnificent Valley of Rocks with its rugged stone pinnacles towering above the sea. Our old map showed the route to Woody Bay as a track but it already had a tarmac surface and today can be a busy coastal road. The coast now reverted to the typical Exmoor seaside scene of slow rolling moors ending abruptly in a line of big hogsback hills dropping suddenly and steeply into the sea.

Returning to the tops after a hot lunch at the Hunter's Inn Hotel in the bottom of the Heddon Valley, we followed the gentle slope offered by a side valley and this led to a farmyard. Our uncertainty about whether we might be trespassing, a very common problem at that period, was put to rest by an apparent local with a surprising North American accent. He set us on the right track for Combe Martin, a straggling nondescript place, reminiscent of the old coal mining towns of the Midlands.

For a time our walking ended here. It was a Sunday and, as usual at that period, the town was fast asleep. While waiting for a bus to take us to Ilfracombe, we were nobbled by a lonely old gentleman with a red face, an impressive white moustache and an old fashioned expansive waistcoat adorned by a large silver watch and chain. Unable to escape from him, we were obliged to listen to a long catalogue of recent minor changes to the local scene.

Exmoor had detained us longer than intended and we were now in a hurry to reach Lands End. Hitch-hiking was at best unpredictable and it took us nearly one and a half days to reach St Ives. For a large part of the way we were given a lift by a sad lonely holidaymaker in an old Austin Seven. Near Hayle, a row of palm trees, backed by white sand and a deep blue sea, together created an exotic scene which neither of us had thought possible in England.

From St Ives we planned a clockwise walk around the Lands End peninsula, stopping one night in Penzance and another at St Just. Since our Spalding days, Norman had become a great camera enthusiast and St Ives proved to be just too photogenic for him to leave in a hurry. With a harbour full of small fishing vessels set against a backdrop of quaint streets and stone buildings, there were many other prowling photographers around only too ready to engage in technical conversations. As a consequence the start of our walk was much delayed.

The Lands End peninsula is a single block of granite

separated from the rest of England by a valley from St Ives to Mounts Bay. We did manage to climb the first high ground of this peninsula for a panoramic view, but after that all the many tracks and paths shown on our map proved to be overgrown by thick bracken and in the end we were obliged to take to the main road. Frustrated and irritable, we clumped along the tarmac watching Mounts Bay and St Michael's Mount slowly unfold into view. A large rusty hulk lay on the shore not far from the Mount. Later we discovered that these were the remains of the famous battleship *HMS Warspite* which had served the country well during the recent war. Finally, in the cool of evening, we entered Penzance and soon found digs for the night in a working class district close to the railway station.

On a fine but hazy and dull morning we set out along the coast towards Lands End. The first attractive spot was Mousehole. Its fishing boats were already gone but had been replaced by a new catch. Numerous tourists were wandering around, taking in the view and frequently snapping their cameras. However, one corner of this scene provided both a sharp contrast and a reminder of the recent past. Seated along a bench, several whiskered old salts, wearing their traditional fishermans' caps and blue jerseys, were engaged in very serious council.

From here we were obliged to follow roads until rejoining the coast again at Porthcurno. This part of inland Cornwall proved flat, bleak and bare with stone walled fields and occasional windswept grey stone villages. Although the sea was only a short distance away on almost every side, there was surprisingly no sense of its presence.

On returning to the cliff top, a fitful sun had emerged to light up a small sandy bay, a headland and a calm blue sea. The water was clear, with the silvery sand on its bottom visible for some distance from the shore, making a pleasing contrast to the once familiar muddy estuaries and often opaque sea of our youth.

A cliff top sign pointed 'To The Theatre'. This led to a copy of an ancient Greek theatre set high above a sea. Surprised and enchanted by the scene, we wondered how often our fickle weather spoiled performances at this exposed spot remote from its Mediterranean origins.

Towards Lands End the bays became fewer and smaller and the cliffs more extensive and impressive. We also encountered the frustrating ins and outs and ups and downs of cliff walking and for long gazed at the large hotel at Lands End before finally reaching it. Although the sun was descending, there were still the crowds who had come in the buses and cars parked at the end of the road. We managed to get into a cafe just as it was about to close. While supping our tea, the people and vehicles outside headed back inland along the bleak open road. With them went all the sounds of chattering and laughter until in the end we were left with Lands End almost to ourselves.

Lands End had proved disappointing because this was not the dramatic promontory which we had imagined, but only a modest bend on the coast. However, in the quiet of evening, I silently saluted this most westerly point of Britain, rejoicing in the many different pleasures which the country had given me in recent times.

The autumn evenings were now drawing in and there was still some way to go to our planned place of rest for the night. A quick march to the north brought us to the quiet little hamlet of Sennen Cove, and a necessary stop for a meal at a café. As we set out again the sun, already a distorted cherry red orb, was about to sink into the Atlantic. We now had two related problems. The first was to find our way through unfamiliar countryside in the approaching darkness and the second was Norman's exhaustion which had reached the stage where he could now only move forward very slowly. The final glimmer went from the sky as we climbed from sand dunes covered in marram grass up to what appeared to be flat tableland. From there, aided by our map, compass and the lights of occasional farm houses gleaming across wide dark spaces, we were eventually very relieved to find a familiar YHA sign and the welcoming bright lights of St Just Youth Hostel. The last walk of that holiday had ended.

From St Just, a combination of bus journeys and hitch-hikes, took us to Helston, Falmouth, Truro and Indian Queens, where after a long frustrating wait we travelled on to Plymouth and Exeter. It was a Friday night and with commercial traffic off the road for two days there would be few lifts. Both of us were now very short of money and we decided to cut our losses and travel overnight by train to Nottingham, a slow journey with many stops and changes at both Bristol and Derby. Throughout that night ticket collectors seemed to be forever waking us from brief comfortless dozes with demands to see our tickets.

It was to be thirty years before I returned to Exmoor and I have never been back to Lands End.

Norman and I had enjoyed each other's company again, but the three years separation after seven close years together at school had taken us off in different directions. It was to be almost another decade before we again reunited and by then we both had young families.

CHAPTER SIX

SOUTH WESTERN INTERLUDES

Walkers often have enjoyable encounters not usually associated with their pastime. One type of encounter is with events different from those experienced in their everyday lives and the other is with unusual and often interesting people. The main reason for the latter is that walkers are readily identifiable by their dress and this often opens the door to immediate communication between strangers, and because a walker is here today and gone tomorrow, the revelations which follow often tend to be less inhibited than usual. Two examples of these encounters, one with an event and the other with a person, took place during the trip which Norman and I made to the South West in 1951. Both now have more than a touch of nostalgia about them.

AN EVENING AT LYNMOUTH

On arriving at Lynmouth following my walk from Minehead, I met Norman as planned. After several hectic days of travel we decided to stay in this most delectable spot for two nights. For that first evening some restful entertainment also seemed appropriate and on enquiry we learnt that there was a choice between a cinema performance up at Lynton and a live summer show at the small pavilion beside the shore. In the event we chose the latter mainly, I think, because it was a new experience for us. In our ignorance we did not contemplate that the show was going to be anything but restful.

The 'Frivolities' show that evening turned out to be the last of that summer season. We paid our half crowns (12.5p) at the entrance and entered a room which, typical of the seaside architecture of the previous century, bore some resemblance to a greenhouse. The seats ranged along a sort of gallery at the back were already occupied by a crowd of noisy youngsters and those in the main body of the hall were filling up with two types of people. There were confident locals familiar with their surroundings and with some other members of the audience and a second type, consisting of holiday visitors, who were generally clustered together in small family groups.

Then the piano tinkled to let everyone know that the performance was about to begin. After an interval for the audience to settle down, a small curtain drew back to reveal the entire star-spangled company. There were five of them. With artificial smiles on their faces and songs from their lips they each introduced themselves in turn. Their combined noise was loud and the discord palpable. Latecomers about to enter the auditorium were even observed to wince visibly before gaining sufficient courage to move forward to their seats. By now both Norman and I were realising that this was not going to be the restful evening which we had hoped for and were apprehensively waiting for revelations to come.

Drawing on long experience, the performers broke the ice by inviting the audience to sing community songs with them. Then they introduced a spirit of competition by getting one half of the audience to render one song and the other a different one. The resulting racket nearly lifted the roof off and the poor seagulls, who normally roosted peacefully above in the quiet of evening, would have had a very nasty shock.

The crowd was now relaxed, ready to listen to the performers and where appropriate to join in with them.

The star of the show was a little rotund North Country comedian whose intense physical activity and rapid changes of outrageous suits more than compensated for his tired jokes. The lead singer was a lady, perhaps past the bloom of youth but still in fine voice. Unfortunately, her renditions were accompanied by very ugly facial expressions. The company, considering its small size, then went on to display amazing versatility with a song and dance act, a recitation, musical interludes and even acrobatics. The high point was a North Devon version of South Sea music and dance complete with grass skirts.

By now the audience were revelling in it all. On this last night of the season an end of term atmosphere prevailed. It seemed that, as there would be no more shows until the next year, now was the time to take every advantage of the present. Already the initial disagreeable impact made by the small unprepossessing stage and the sad looking curtains had been lost in the stir of events. Norman and I, two shy and rather reserved young men at the best of times, had relaxed and were enjoying ourselves. However our comforting sense of security was mistaken and we were totally unprepared for what was to happen next.

The lead comedian, aided and abetted by other members of the troupe, then went on to introduce a series of party games involving the audience. Norman and I, even among our small group of friends in former times, always tended to shuffle off unobtrusively into inconspicuous corners whenever anything of this nature was abroad. But now we were trapped in the middle of an audience with no means of escape without drawing attention to ourselves. During the long stressful period which followed there were moments when I would have gladly disappeared under my seat if that been physically possible.

Volunteers were called for the first game and fortunately a sufficient number came from the audience. This entailed sitting in a row of chairs on the stage and singing comic songs in turn. For the next and later games the flow of volunteers quickly dried up and then members of the audience were coerced by the company to come forward. The most pernicious method was a modified form of "pass the parcel". Sealed envelopes were passed up and down the rows while the piano beat out a suitable rhythm matching the very high speed with which the object moved from person to person. Then when the music stopped the poor unfortunate left holding this object had to go up onto the stage, open the envelope and perform the instruction within. Horror upon horror, these ranged from making disgusting animal noises to receiving small but embarrassingly rude presents. I do not think there can be any doubt that Norman and I broke the envelope-handling speed record. The show continued with a beer-guzzling competition, a balloon bursting race, a knobbly knee contest and finally a competition for the girl with the best legs. At long last both of us relaxed, sat upright and took careful note. After a close scrutiny of the contestants limbs we both agreed that the semi-finalist really should have won. When the contest was over and the participants were returning to their seats, we tried to identify the owner of those lovely legs but could not agree to whom they belonged.

The show was now approaching the finale. On this last night, in a ceremony somewhat reminiscent of a school prize-giving, each member of the company was showered with flowers and gifts. Only one final deed remained. A solemn, serious, and portly gentleman dressed in a brown suit, who had been sitting on the front row, probably the local councillor responsible for entertainments, arose with slow dignity, grasped the lapels of his suit jacket with his hands and gave a ponderous unimaginative vote of thanks to the rather down at heel curtains directly in front of him. When he announced that this season's show had been a success, the little comedian, standing to one side but in full view of the audience, exaggeratedly pulled his empty pockets from out of his trousers. The loud outburst from the crowd which followed drew the attention of the speaker to the comedian. Clearly irritated by the cheeky interruption, he gave the latter a dark scowl. The little man, realising that he gone too far in poking fun at Authority, made an immediate contrite apology but the incident put a distinct dampener on the end of the show. Then, with immaculate timing, the pianist launched into the National Anthem before anyone could leap up and make a precipitate departure from the hall.

The old pavilion still stands but I have the impression that shows of this type have not taken place here for many years.

The following night was our last in Lynmouth and we stopped for a farewell drink at the old pub beside the harbour. It was a Saturday evening and, as the landlord did not quieten the sounds of revelry within, we went outside to sit on the stone parapet above lively river water swirling past grounded boats in the harbour. The moonlight made Lynmouth enchanting, tracing a silvery path across the sea and lighting up the star strewn sky beyond the nearby high dark hills. High above us the lights of scattered hotels gleaming out from this shadowy mass seemed to be suspended in space. Overcome by this romantic scene we both agreed that this would be an ideal place for a honeymoon. However when the time came neither of us came here with our new wives.

NEWTH

After our long tiring walk from St Ives, we arranged

bed and breakfast at a terraced house in one of the back streets near Penzance railway station. The transaction was conducted with the lady of the house and we did not meet her husband until later that evening. He proved to be an elderly bright eyed individual whose brisk manner belied his age. From the start it was obvious that he welcomed any opportunity to talk to newcomers and conducted the conversation for nearly all the evening. He began by politely enquiring about the parts of the country which we had passed through and what our thoughts were about them and then went on to investigate our future itinerary.

However, this polite interchange was merely a warm up for the main event, a monologue on his former career. It transpired that he had been a pioneer of the early cinema. To put this subject into its contemporary context, by the early 1950s the cinema was at the peak of its popularity and for most of the younger generation it had been and still was the only form of entertainment which they had known. Almost every town had more than one cinema and the decor of these institutions was often contrived to create a sense of luxury, so that both the buildings and the films shown within them provided a temporary escape from the often harsh reality of life during the war years and the austere period which followed. Admittedly I had once seen a television set, but that had a small blue flickering screen and was placed in a special room all by itself in the Science Museum in South Kensington. In these circumstances it was not surprising that anything to do with cinemas and the cinema industry caught and held our attention.

Our host, whose name turned out to be Newth, went on to tell us that the cinema had been known as the moving bioscope in its early days and had moved from place to place around the country. Somewhat to our surprise in view of its current esteem, he then went on to tell us that cinema shows were not held in high regard, being no more than side shows at travelling fairs. He also spoke of the moving pictures of Edwardian times, the most popular apparently being that of Bleriot crossing the English coast at Dover after making the first aeroplane flight over the English Channel. Although the sequence was apparently little more than flickering black shadows on a lighter background, it never failed to raise audiences to a fever pitch of excitement. In the current period immediately after the massive air campaigns of the Second World War, all this seemed very ancient history to us. But here was a lively man talking about this and other similar events as though they had taken place only yesterday.

Then the word "fairs" immediately led our host into a whole new subject. With flashing eyes and animated gestures he described the splendours of the highly decorated transportable side shows, the joys of the steam engines which powered the attractions and the music produced by the old steam organs. We also heard accounts of fat ladies, a man who could use his feet like hands, the "ossified" Russian who was transparent and many more freaks. Then for the first time that evening his tone became more serious as he went on to deplore the attitude of young people who nowadays were only attracted to fairs by the thrill of having their stomachs turned over!

Up to this point the lady of the house had kept silent, the only sound emanating from her direction being the clicking of her knitting needles. Then when London happened to be mentioned she suddenly sprang to life and surprisingly took over the conversation with an animated account of the pleasures of London's street markets, ranging from Petticoat Lane to Portobello Road, places which I had to admit having never visited during my years there. During this part of the conversation we learnt that Newth was now a shopkeeper and that his business was located a short distance up the street.

The conversation, or more correctly our hosts' monologues, continued to a late hour before our hostess firmly brought the proceedings to an end. Even so, pertinent questions about the couple remained unanswered. How was it that a man, who had travelled all over the country for many years and had an intimate knowledge of many towns and cities, finished up in the most westerly town in the land? Had he failed to move with the times and then been forced to follow increasingly remote fair circuits as permanent cinemas sprung up in every town? The only certainty was that Newth still longed for his early days on the road.

As next day's walk was long, we were in a hurry to get away. However that did not stop our host from showing us photographs of old time fairs with their portable structures of amazing intricacy and ornamentation and, while we were consuming our eggs and bacon, he also entertained us with a collection of music hall tunes on a concertina.

In spite of this hurry, we could not resist the temptation to take a look at our host's shop before finally leaving the neighbourhood. It was on a corner a little way down the street and bore the legend 'Newth - General Stores'. However, the window was filled with a dusty collection of old musical instruments, party games, false moustaches and false noses.

CHAPTER SEVEN

NATIONAL SERVICE OPPORTUNITIES

I did not look forward to my two year's National Service with much pleasure. However, at least in part, I rationalised it as due payment for the excellent free education which the State had given me. Long before I had accepted a necessary need to bear arms for my country. This was not based on the old fashioned terms of 'For God, King and Country', words sometimes seen emblazoned on Great War memorials, with priorities presumably in that order, but for my country alone. My definition of Country, although inclusive of the whole, was primarily concerned with its hills, mountains, moors, woods and coasts. Much to my dismay I had recently discovered that large parts of this countryside were shut off by blocked paths and tracks, erroneous 'Keep Out' signs and misleading 'advice' from landowners or their agents.

This attitude towards bearing arms had evolved long before and had much to do with one government wartime poster. This depicted a South Downs scene which, for me, banished in the Fens at the time, had become a place of great longing. The poster showed sunlit rounded green slopes dropping away into a valley where a venerable farmhouse was protected by tall trees. Sea glinted in the distance and in the foreground an old shepherd stood with his crook, dog and flock. Beneath were the words 'This is your Britain, fight for it NOW'. Although the war was now over, this potent image remained in my mind, especially as access to much of our countryside had still to be won.

Fortunately, this was one of the quieter periods of Britain's post World War Two military involvement. The savage Korean War was coming to an end and apart from this there was only the rubber planters' war with communist guerrillas in Malaya. However, Russia had recently attempted to starve Berlin into submission and a few years after my full time National Service, the chronic problem of the Suez Canal Zone degenerated into armed conflict. Although only a minority of National Servicemen were called upon to fight, war was a constant possibility and conscripts needed to be mentally prepared for this eventuality. However I have to say that my circumstances were very different from those of my father who, as an eighteen year old conscript, had marched into the deadly chaos of the Western Front during the major German spring offensive in 1918.

Access to the countryside, although still far from perfect, is now much better than in the 1940s and 1950s. Then, few walked in the great outdoors and consequently government gave them little consideration. Today's huge number of walkers have a much more powerful voice in the land, not least because many rural communities have come to depend on them for a livelihood.

I entered the RAF as a conscript aircraftman at the notorious Padgate recruit camp. After seven hectic but nonetheless interesting months of training, service life became more relaxing in circumstances where responsibility proved to be minimal. When my final posting came it was not to some remote British outpost or the more likely destinations of Germany and the Suez Canal Zone, but to Weeton Camp in the Fylde of Lancashire.

Even during the initial training period, I took the opportunity of a long weekend's leave for a trip to the Shropshire Hills with the Curlews. It proved another happy discovery. Here ancient hard rocks, split in two by an ancient fault, suddenly rear up from a wide gentle plain. The Long Mynd, a heathery plateau with numerous deep valleys let into its sides stands to the west, and to the east rounded hills culminate in the craggy fastness of Caer Caradoc. Since then, this small but choice area has remained one of my favourite mini-regions.

During the summer of 1952 I took advantage of my improved pay of nine shillings a day, two weeks leave and a travel warrant supplied by the RAF to join Peter of the Curlews on a holiday in the Scottish Highlands. It was my first trip to the land of my mother's forebears.

The beginning of that holiday followed a typical tourist pattern with a climb up Ben Nevis and so did the end, with boat trips, including one around Mull. But the middle was unforgettably unique, presenting a total change from my everyday world. A bus of utility design and poor springing carried us westwards, together with mail, provisions and groceries, from Invergarry on the first leg of the journey to Loch Hourn. Civilisation was soon left behind and apart from a brief stop at a hydroelectric construction camp, the surroundings became wild, large and very empty. Tarmac gave way to a stony track at Tomdoun and the increased jolting made it all but impossible to enjoy the mirror-like water of Loch Quoich and distant blue mountains crowned with white clouds. Above all else I was struck by the great spaciousness of the Highlands.

The bus journey ended at Glenquioch Lodge where we relaxed for a time in pervasive stillness beside gently lapping loch water. Then a decrepit car with blue smoke issuing from its exhaust arrived to take us on to Kinloch Hourn. The driver, our host to be, initially made some effort to be friendly but soon reverted to his natural uncommunicative dourness. During our entire stay at

Kinloch Hourn, the only statements he ever volunteered were to the effect that Westminster was far away and that the local heavy rainfall was vital to prevent his sheep meadows from becoming deserts of sand. Consequently there were no answers to many intriguing puzzles encountered on our subsequent wanderings. Throughout our stay his wife was only seen at a distance.

The journey continued westwards, now through intimate rugged country during which nearby stream directions changed from east to west. A deserted crofter's cottage was followed by a canyon, and then the head of Loch Hourn appeared ahead, a narrow strip of blue sea hemmed in by high mountains. Our destination, a solitary farm, stood on a small area of flat meadow land beside its head waters.

That afternoon set a pattern for the rest of our stay. We followed a ruinous path along the south side of the upper loch to what disappointingly proved to be deserted settlements at Skiary and Runival because Skiary was shown as an existing village on our map. Only one dwelling showed signs of recent occupation and this added to our growing sense of detachment from the outside world. The same map showed the Loch eventually broadening where it was joined by Glen Barrisdale and that this second valley might be populated. Further downstream the village of Arnisdale stood on the side of the Loch where it widened towards the Sound of Sleat. We planned to visit both places during the days ahead.

From our present position at the head of the Loch there was no indication of where the land eventually gave way to open sea. In its expected direction high pointed peaks reared up into the sky, and being unable to pronounce Gaelic names, they became known to us as the Pyramid Mountains. In this sunny peaceful world the only sounds came from the tide gently slurping across seaweed beds, coloured pebbles, shells and sand and from a distant stream hurrying down a mountain side. Tempted by the warm incoming water, I paddled while Peter lay sprawled out asleep on a nearby grassy hummock. As the sun moved lower and the shadows grew longer, the enclosing mountains seemed to close in on us.

Next day the weather was dull, cloudy and muggy. We climbed through unexpected eucalyptus trees above a hunting lodge to reach a hilly plateau and a new cool breeze. The well engineered path, presumably built for deer stalkers, contrasted with the wild desolation all around. Beyond a lonely lochan, where water-lilies bloomed along its edge and an attendant heron remained undisturbed by our presence, we went up into cold thick cloud and stopped.

Hoping for improved weather we sat down and waited. Far below winding Loch Hourn passed into and out of sight at intervals, with the sites of Runival and Skiary appearing as tiny deltas of a lighter green. A promising patch of brighter sky appeared seawards above a saddle in the mountains but was soon replaced by dark shadow, a pattern that was to be repeated several times. It eventually became apparent that the seaside, some miles away, was enjoying fine weather which would never come our way. At that we called it a day and retreated back to the farm. During the whole of the time we neither saw nor heard any sign of other humans.

Next morning overnight rain had passed away, but clouds were still low. Come what may we decided to take a challenging walk to Barrisdale over the mountains and return along the coast. On passing Skiary, we noticed the bones of a boat on the shore which time had given the same colour as surrounding boulders. Then while clambering over the remains of a croft wall, a halfpenny fell out of my pocket and lodged in a crevice. On impulse I left it there to reclaim on some future date which has never come.

The weather was pleasant at loch level but became muggy and hot on the climb up the mountain. Thick grass, bracken and heather, all sodden after the overnight rain soon soaked our socks and boots. Short stretches of deer track sometimes proved helpful, but it was only on reaching a stream cascading over a succession of rock ledges that the going became easier. Then, as the slope became less steep, we entered thick, dark and very wet Scotch mist. Our bodies were soon so soaked by perspiration and precipitation that wetness did not matter any more. Therein lay potential danger, for tiredness and discomfort can lead to carelessness and possible accidents. We also needed to stay close together in that poor visibility because, once separated, Peter's deafness would have made contact difficult to re-establish. Ignoring unreliable intuition telling us to go in a direction other than that indicated by our compasses, we came to the brink of a void. Many years later I was reminded of this day on reading about a lone walker who had lost his life on these hills in a fall and that some time elapsed before his body was eventually found. However, on that day we had a stroke of luck. The thick mist cleared momentarily to reveal part of Glen Barrisdale ahead and, more importantly, that the way down to it, although steep, appeared feasible. Around a thousand feet further down we came to the first small gnarled tree and from there could just make out a river bend ahead. Then the mist curtain suddenly drew aside and the whole Glen Barrisdale came into view together with the welcome sign of a path down the valley. But behind and above us thick mist still blanketed the mountain side.

While Peter and I were photographing a waterfall, a Highlander on horseback, driving three cows, suddenly passed by. Wearing a Sherlock Holmes hat, a green tweed plus four suit, and carrying a large telescope, he sat in a slumped position on his mount and seemed totally unaware of our presence. However, after we had regained the path he turned round to take a good look at us. We waved in return but there was no response.

At first the surroundings remained wild, with striated rocks littering a valley floor enclosed by tall rugged hills. Ahead the now close Pyramid Mountains, massive and black with their tops still shrouded in cloud, seemed to hold a terrible fascination. A sharp rise in the path brought our first view of the outer loch where, in complete contrast, sky, water and distant mountains were all bright blue. At first the mind could not accept the shock of this blaze of colour after hours of dullness. Ahead the now flat glen bottom ended in broad dazzling white sands along the bay. Two small dwellings, a deserted croft and a house were now in view but there were no more signs of humans. Then a seemingly English country lane, with trees along its sides and dandelions flowering below in the greensward, led us on to the white sands where our boots inadvertently crushed some of the multitudinous delicate white seashells.

A ruined simple church stood at the entrance to inner Loch Hourn with its roof slates scattered over a wide area. With our clothing and boots having long since dried out, we luxuriated for a time in sunshine on a grassy bank. Away in the distance some of Skye's higher blue mountains still retained their crowns of white cloud. The old coastal path, once well made with parapets along its rocky parts and embankments across the boggy ones, was now covered in heather and disintegrating. Finally, we sat again for a while above the deserted homestead of Runival and its pasture, thinking that on a lovely warm evening such as this it would have been hard for the former inhabitants to abandon their lovely home. Back at the farm the tide had reached up to the meadows where long shadows highlighted nibbling sheep. We were now late for dinner which once again consisted of generous helpings of carrots and mutton.

Next morning the outside world was dark, gloomy and very wet, so we delayed our departure, hoping that something better might soon come along. The lounge was dark and depressing, shut in by mountains and trees and dominated by a large picture of the disastrous Great War Battle of Loos. Reading matter was confined to a bible, biblical novels, and several Sir Walter Scott novels, but the badly needed information about Loch Hourn and its history was totally lacking. Around midday the rain ceased and we ventured out, promising that on this day we would avoid all wet undergrowth and bogs. Thus our only option was to follow the track by which we had arrived. Beyond small waterfalls the valley then widened to a lochan and a recently deserted croft which provided shelter when rain again came tumbling down. All its former homeliness had gone and soon the roof would be off, just like all those other deserted crofts we had encountered.

The rain ceased again and we set off up the track to the watershed where streams began to flow eastwards towards Loch Quioch. This place was memorable for the only friendly encounter during our entire stay at Kinloch Hourn. It came in the form of a slim middle-aged Lowlander with grey hair, clad in the upper half of a suit and rolled up grey flannel trousers. He was pushing an ordinary bicycle along.

With bursting enthusiasm he announced 'I took the ferry from Mallaig to Inverie this morning, then crossed over the mountains to Barrisdale before walking round the coast to the farm where I had an excellent tea.'

Breathlessly, he then added 'I'm about to rush off to

Tomdoun to see if I can spend the night there.'

Before we could get a word in edgeways, he glanced at his machine, ejaculating 'The heather has cleaned all the dirt off my cycle chain!'

With that he dashed off, pushing the bicycle beside him, and was soon out of sight around a bend. We were astonished, not only by this sudden interlude among all the surrounding emptiness, but also by his notable achievement, bearing in mind the distance he had covered, the added handicap of his bicycle, the very wet state of the countryside and the thick heather along most of the way. Back at the farm we could clearly see his tyre tracks and foot marks trailing back through the heather.

Next day was our last at Kinloch Hourn so we decided to take a look at Arnisdale, retracing part of our first walk. On the plateau, now visibly surrounded by lofty mountains, the rain came tumbling down in swift sharp showers. Constantly changing light created scenes redolent of those once popular Victorian oil paintings of the Highlands while at our feet, heather, orchids and other small mountain flowers bloomed in profusion. The watershed was a small hillock and from here the path dropped steeply into Glen Arnisdale's rocky sides. Predictably in these parts, the first signs of civilisation came as ruined cottages, some little more than heaps of stones. But one had surviving gable ends with amusingly similar bushes growing out of each of its two chimneys.

Beyond two lochans the mountain sides closed in to create a rocky ravine, the most craggy scene of our stay. Here raw rock walls plunged straight down into a churning river as a series of zigzags took us to the plain below. During the descent I happened to look back to see my first Highland deer perched on a lofty crag against the sky. Then the distant view widened to reveal the blue water of outer Loch Hourn with sunny blue mountains beyond.

At first the plain was bracken covered, but beyond a high fence there were pastures with sheep and cattle. Here the soft brush of long grass against our bare legs reminded us of home as did the sight of dandelions and clover in flower.

Corran was a handful of well maintained cottages where absolute quiet reigned. The nearby village of Arnisdale consisted of two dozen homes ranged in a single line around a curving bay. Apart from Arnisdale House, these were simple structures built of stone and faced with plaster, as were both the school and church. Set only a few feet above the water, they made a pleasing sight until the eye rested on to the narrow pebble beach littered with bottles, tins and all manner of flotsam. Chickens scratched around a few small boats, most of which were falling into decay. The fronts of the dwellings were pleasingly decorated with flowers and honeysuckle and one even had some hydrangeas which immediately reminded me of far-off Somerset of the year before. But the bulky mountain looming behind could never have been in England.

Our lunch place was a patch of greensward overlooking a small island and, apart from a few squabbling seagulls, pervasive peace reigned. Two men with a cow had said good morning to us on approach to the village, but after that there had been no signs of life, apart from a distant car leaving the settlement by the only road out of the village, the chickens on the beach, the sea birds and a dog which had growled at our approach.

Returning, the village street seemed as quiet and empty as before. A prickly feeling on the back of my neck caused me to turn round and now see a man in an open doorway looking at us. Alerted, I again turned to see somebody else peering from behind another part-closed house door. Then we both turned around to see a curtain suddenly dropping back into place. This reaction to our presence was unique for both of us and we began to feel most uncomfortable. On reaching the beginning of the village street, we finally encountered three middle-aged men. Two continued their conversation but at least the third did acknowledge our greeting. After a few steps, in what had now become a regular pattern, we turned around again. All three were standing still staring at us.

By the end of that day we were glad to reach Kinloch Hourn after a walk of more than twenty miles over the hills. On the next day our journey back to the outside world began.

Over fifty years later, I wonder what has happened to this superb, strange and unforgettable region. Did it remain as we found it, or did the evident long decline continue? Or have holiday developments, which have now irrevocably changed so many beautiful places, reached out to this remote part of our island? It would be interesting to know.

On arrival, Weeton turned out to be a bleak hutted camp of World War Two vintage, but there were advantages. It was only a short distance from my much loved Lakes and the North Pennines which I had yet to explore. Blackpool was also just down the road.

The first tangible sign of an enjoyable future came on a bright, cold morning shortly after my arrival. As Orderly Officer of the day I was marching around the bleak regimented wooden huts when I suddenly happened upon an open spot which presented a view across the flat land of the Fylde and across the waters of Morecambe Bay to bright, snow-covered Black Combe, the first big Lakeland hill, and hints of higher white peaks beyond. This unexpected scene not only provided joy on that day but also held great promise for the future.

Whenever my finances permitted, from that time

onwards I shot up to the Lakes. Some trips were with RAF colleagues and later I joined the local Fylde Mountaineering Club. Over the seasons I became familiar with the individual shape of each mountain and the ways up and down. With few walkers abroad in those days, the paths were not always clear cut, very different from today's obvious scars across many Lakeland scenes. The affection and respect engendered on my first visit to these hills in 1951 were now reinforced by snowy experiences during that first winter at Weeton.

When short of money I sometimes wandered around the nearby Fylde, a flat area unlike any other that I had known because it was pitted with strange grass covered hollows, probably relics of the Ice Ages. Alternatively, a short bus ride took me to Blackpool with its sea front, amusement parks and piers, reminders of my early pleasures at Skegness, and providing more grown-up ones in the form of the girls I met at the Tower Ballroom.

Another short bus ride inland led to very different pleasures. The small town of Garstang was not far from an isolated outlier of the Pennines which I knew as the Bowland Fells. It was one of those understated regions, discovered almost by accident and over time came to love. Although not a loner by nature I am happy to take solitary walks in the countryside if no like-minded companions are around, for the lack of human companionship is often balanced by intimate contact with nature. On one occasion, as I shall recount later, that intimate contact proved all too much.

By this time I had acquired some old fashioned heavy camping equipment. At one peaceful place in these hills, two becks came together at a level patch of close-cropped grass beneath steep heathery moorland. Sometimes I camped here, listening to tinkling water, the sharp strange sounds of night and birdsong at dawn. Pleasures also included heating a late night drink crouched over a small cooker with only blackness and distant stars beyond and the joy of walking through fresh morning dew with bare feet. Never did another soul come by. One winter's day, after a windy tramp over these hills, I learnt that the nearby Larne-Stranraer ferry had been sunk in the gale. Then news started to come through of the sea surge which had flooded many parts of the East Coast. My home village was one of the victims and on that day its coast was changed forever.

Perhaps my most treasured memory of the Bowland Fells is one which came as a complete surprise. Two years before I had walked with the Curlews in the Three Peaks, climbing the lovely spacious peaks of Ingleborough and Pen-y-Ghent, once thought to have been the highest mountains in England. Due to the differing terrains, I had overlooked their proximity to my present position. Then while traversing a boggy moor one winter's afternoon, concentrating on the slippery dark peat at my feet, I momentarily looked up. There above the immediate dark shadowed surroundings, a distant Ingleborough had appeared in the low afternoon sun, startling pink against a clear cold blue sky. It was breathtaking in its simple purity. As I gradually discovered more of my own country, the number of hills yet to be explored seemed increasingly endless.

In some respects I was sorry when my carefree National Service days came to an end, but I also recognised the need to be getting on with my life. On my final Lakeland trip before release a snowy walk took me over the hills to the east of Ullswater. At the start of the return journey the coach made a refreshment stop at the inn on the top of Kirkstone Pass. Not being over fond of such places, I wandered outside. Night had already come, but a full moon shining on the many snow patches spread over the tops created a dazzling silvery display, heightened by areas of dark shade in between. The stark contrast accentuated the wild scene in a manner that I had never experienced before. For a long time I stood out there in the cold, transposing it to memory. My thoughts at that moment were mixed, joy for all the pleasure that the Lakes had recently given me and sadness that I might not return for a long time. Two years before a similar Lakeland goodbye had proved to be mistaken but this time around the gap would be a long one.

CHAPTER EIGHT

FEAR

As mentioned previously, I became familiar with the nearby gentle lonely hills on the west side of the Pennines during my first winter and spring at Weeton Camp. At this distance in time I do not recall whether the summer which followed was a good one or not but, on one particular day when I decided to walk on them, it was sunny, hazy and exceptionally hot, just the sort of weather when one welcomed escape from the heat and boredom of service life to the anticipated cool freedom of the hills. Contrary to expectations, as I climbed to the tops heat and haze increased. By the time I had reached the broad plateau, the visibility had become so poor that I was obliged to set my compass and walk along its bearing. Up to this point I had been enjoying myself, but the pleasure was not going to last much longer.

At first almost imperceptibly and then with increasing speed, the daylight failed until my surroundings had been transformed from bright sunshine to one of sinister dark shadow. Simultaneously, the world about me had suddenly become very quiet, as if waiting apprehensively for something terrible to happen. In this weird silence the only sounds were those of my own breathing and the steady clump of my boots on the rough dry surface of the moor. From past experience I should have long since expected to have heard the sound of thunder, but there was none and its absence added to my unease. Some time before common sense had warned me to turn back but innate stubbornness had driven me on. Now I was regretting my stupidity.

Then blackness, as dark as that of a moonless night, suddenly descended without warning and even my feet were barely visible. Yet the uncanny silence still prevailed. Unease had now been replaced by fear, due in part to the unnatural change that had taken place and to the incomprehensible ones yet to come.

I did not have long to wait. A sighing breeze came suddenly out of nowhere and within seconds had waxed into a raging gale. Simultaneously, the former enveloping opacity was swept aside like a curtain to reveal a new sharp green light shining eerily up from below. This illuminated the underside of a huge black cloud which stretched away from my head across the flat land of the Fylde towards the sea and far beyond. But this was no ordinary cloud for the mass was in violent convulsion and so were the innumerable green and yellow tentacles from its underside which frantically clawed downwards. To my now terrified irrational mind these seemed to be attempting to pull the earth up into the sky. Words cannot adequately describe the scene, except to liken it to an old artist's conception of Judgement Day. But this was no unmoving silent work of art from which one could choose to turn away, but an inescapable scene alive with buffeting wind and tortured motion.

Having registered this image, I panicked. Here I was, a solitary figure standing on a high almost flat plateau with all hell let loose above me and no obvious means of escape. And escape at that moment was my only coherent thought. If it had been possible to burrow myself in the ground I would gladly have done so. Instead all I could do was turn and run, but at least there was sufficient residual sense to head away in the direction where the hill first fell away towards lower ground. Bounding over peat and tussocks on that crazy rout my breath was soon reduced to anguished sobs and at the same time my inadequate rubberised Service ground sheet, suspended around my neck, flapped up and down like the broken wings of a bird. The gale continued unabated and after what seemed to be an interminable age, it finally brought lightning, thunder, rain and hail. In other circumstances my reaction would have been different, but now I welcomed them as recognisable phenomena of a familiar world. These changes also brought the hurt of hail on my exposed head, arms and legs, but for once it went almost unnoticed.

After a seemingly endless age, which in reality may have only been a matter of minutes, I collided with solid objects on that otherwise featureless plain. These were the remains of an old stone wall. My immediate reaction was one of great relief for here was something not created by Nature in a terrible and unpredictable rage, but by the human race to which I belonged. With lungs on the point of bursting, legs aching, a body soaked with water and with vision badly distorted by rain streaked spectacles, I grasped the rasping grit stones. Their physical protection was minimal but the mental one enormous, for here at last was something that was not totally alien.

Never before or since have I known a similar torrent and it continued long after the thunder and lightning had moved on. All the earlier heat of the day had now gone and, as I crouched against the poor shelter provided by the stones, my once overheated body cooled down until hands and feet grew cold and the chill began to extend to my core. It was time to get up and go. The downpour may have now eased to that of a very wet day but this was of no importance because my soaking was total. Instinctively I followed the ruined stone wall because it had been my protector and must eventually lead to civilisation. At length it turned away from the plateau top and downhill.

Moorland became rough pasture, and it was here, contrary to all expectations, that two figures came into view. My instinct was to rush up to them with an emotional greeting but the rules of conventional behaviour between strangers had already taken over. The two equally wet bedraggled lads and I exchanged mutual banalities about the weather and then went our separate ways. My route led to the village of Chipping where I first caught a bus to Preston and then another back to the camp. That journey was slow, cold and very uncomfortable.

Pondering on the events of that day, I realised that they had taught me two lessons, the first about the superhuman power of nature and the second about my own patent frailty. Except for one colleague, I did not recount my experiences in any detail back at the camp, primarily because of personal embarrassment. That exception was a sincere Christian and after listening to my tale with great interest he proffered the opinion that I had undergone a profound religious experience. Taken aback, I could only demur in very general terms. The truth was that I did not wish to hurt his feelings by stating that the encounter had given me an insight into the world of vulnerable primitive man confronted by his terrible and unpredictable god of nature.

Since that day I have walked many thousands of miles and have never encountered similar storms. However, it must be said that since then I have always been cautious about where I go when thunderstorms are threatening!

I have never returned to those hills. It is not that I have been unwilling but other priorities always seemed to have got in the way, notably my nearby much-loved Lake District. However, when travelling north along the M6, I always remember to seek out the soft profile of those hills along the eastern horizon and give a passing thought to that day long ago.

CHAPTER NINE

TIME OUT

Following my release from the RAF, I stayed with my parents in Nottingham for a short time before taking up my first professional job with a major oil company. On earlier leaves I had occasionally gone to the Saturday night hop in the basement of the city centre YMCA opposite the Victoria Station, and on the second occasion following my release I met a lovely girl with an unusual name. Sunya became a great pal and within a year we were married. I had hoped that my employers might send me to their oil refinery in Cheshire, but instead it was back to the Essex shore of the Thames Estuary where I had been five years before.

Not only was I now a married man, with the responsibilities which that entails, but was also far removed from high hills. My walking was confined to striding to work across flat grassy marshes and at weekends tramping down lanes along higher ground a mile or so to the north of our bungalow home.

During this period there was only one reminder of my earlier walking days and this made a lasting impression on both of us. Some years before, while standing on the cliffs at Lands End, I had considered this spot to be the last of England in the west. In reality that honour really belonged to a lonely tight cluster of small granite islands set in the Atlantic some twenty eight miles further out. Now the Scillies were our destination.

The start was not auspicious. The recently commissioned 'Scillonian II' initially proceeded westwards under the lee of the Lands End Peninsula. But after this was behind us, the earlier stiff breeze was replaced by a wild wind and a very rough sea. At this juncture I realised why the slate roofs next to our previous night's lodgings in Penzance had been set in cement! All too apparent, we were now crossing a stormy Atlantic in a vessel which was not only of modest size, but also of relatively shallow draught. Thus we were not only subject to violent rolling motions but also to periodic sickening bumps when the vessel's exposed bottom crashed back into the water. Many of the passengers became sick, especially my young wife, who in a weak, woebegone voice, periodically told me that she wished to die. Gavin, our small toddler son, also suffered but remained silent apart from occasional groans. By now I was regretting that we had embarked on this lunatic adventure.

Yet the distress of my small family ended suddenly. Green islands bound by massive golden brown rocks suddenly appeared on our right. Then the Scillonian rounded a headland and, at a stroke, the high wind and heavy seas were replaced by unimaginable calm and, for the first time that day, summer's warmth. My family's rapid return to health was almost as miraculous as the change of surroundings. For the eventual return we dosed ourselves with sea-sickness tablets and predictably the ocean was as calm as a mill pond all the way.

We were drawn to these islands by their famed beauty and because they seemed ideal for a family constrained by a toddler's limited mobility. With a fleet of open boats ferrying passengers to and from the outer islands, only short walks were necessary to reach many very different scenes, ranging from salt-sprayed coastal moorland above rock bastions facing the mighty force of the ocean, to long white sandy beaches backed by sheltered nooks and the tiny hedged enclosures where daffodils were grown. Best of all were the colourful flower displays on every untended patch of ground which had sun, water and shelter. Here wild flowers grew happily next to escaped varieties. Yet only a short distance away around the next corner, there might be bare rock facing a searching wind and the Atlantic's white waves. The sun shone every day, so apart from the dazzling flowers all the other bright colours of Scilly were at their best, ranging from the deep blue of the ocean which, as water became shallower, changed through shades of turquoise to finish on gleaming white sands. At the time this experience seemed dreamlike after several years beside the muddy Thames Estuary. The high point of the holiday came on a calm day when we ventured out as far as the Bishops Rock lighthouse, the most westerly point of England, and on the way back encountered a large basking shark. This glorious array of island scenery restored my enthusiasm for the far South West after the somewhat disappointing Cornish trip of some years before.

We lodged in a small cottage in Hugh Town on St. Mary's, where the old fashioned way of life reminded me of that in my home village during the 1930s. The islanders current grievance was having to pay income tax for the first time. In addition, the few vehicles on St. Mary's were not only ancient but also lacked number plates. It was a holiday that we soon hoped to repeat but fate then took a hand and we did not return for many years.

By the following summer we had acquired a new baby daughter and had been transferred to the Netherlands. Although this country's topography might have been similar to that of the Fens, we were fascinated by its history and for both its similarities to and differences from England. At that time it was necessary to speak Dutch in order to conduct our everyday lives, and we soon found it to be much closer to the old Anglo-Saxon tongue of our ancestors than modern English. Both of us became very fond of the Netherlands and its people and have since always regarded it as our second homeland.

Due to the flat terrain and crowded population, my type of walking was not possible here. Local walking clubs marched in step along roads with one person at the back carrying a rucksack, presumably full of first aid equipment. Most of these groups had individual uniforms, including one with full Scottish Highland regalia. This was never the sort of perambulation which I had in mind!

However, I did enjoy walking along the nearby sandy North Sea shore with its many reminders of the Lincolnshire coast. Grass covered sand dunes stretched all the way from Hoek van Holland in the south to Den Helder in the north, and in the vicinity of The Hague there were also many well maintained meandering paths through the marram grass and rose bushes. On fine days I walked to my office in Scheveningen along a route which took me through some of the city's lovely parks, then along quiet back streets and finally past the harbour which in those days was still the base for a fleet of herring drifters. Then many older ladies in Scheveningen and even some of the younger ones still wore their traditional long black dresses with small white lace caps, from which two large horn-like golden pins protruded.

During the latter part of our stay, I bought a second-hand left hand drive Morris 1000. In this we explored the nearby Continent, especially the hillier parts. The extent of our family walking might have been limited, but my children's efforts made me very proud of them. These Continental hills were often very different from the ones that I had known at home, with their deep winding valleys wandering past hillsides covered by trees in Luxembourg and the Hartz and vineyards in the Rhineland and everywhere fairytale castles crowned high points.

At the end of 1960 I was transferred to London and for the first time was able to live in the Weald, the land of my delight during the 1938 holiday and of happy group rambles more than a decade later. We bought a house in Horley, primarily for its convenient rail connections to central London.

Sadly, a once much loved area can sometimes prove disappointing on return and it was so here. No doubt my tastes had altered to some extent but the reason had more to do with changes to the scene in the interim. Basically, London had spilled outwards, especially into the London-Brighton corridor where we were now living. Nearby Crawley had become a New Town and the adjacent Gatwick Airport was expanding rapidly. Thus a once much loved, peaceful, countryside was becoming busy suburbia. However, there was one most unusual compensation. For the only time in my working life I was able to walk from home along semi-rural footpaths to catch international flights!

There were also occasional trips to the South Downs whose lovely curvaceous green slopes and white cliffs still remained very attractive. My most rewarding outings during this period came on summer evenings after I had returned from work. Far removed from the filthy atmosphere of central London, I was then able to walk rapidly across green meadows in clean fresh air.

Matthew, our second son, arrived halfway through our stay in Surrey and we moved to Wales a year later.

CHAPTER TEN

WALKING ONCE MORE

There was no serious walking for almost a decade, but my slow return to this lifelong addiction can be pinpointed to our stay in South Wales. In between the need to earn a living from an often demanding job, bringing up young children and providing help to ailing parents, there was often little time for personal indulgence. Yet whenever the opportunity arose I grasped it and went out for a walk.

We enjoyed our stay in Swansea, a friendly city set on a wide bay overlooking the sea and backed by hills and mountains. At that time the increasingly frantic rush and bustle of modern urban communities had not yet reached this final big town in the west. Yet my overriding memory of Swansea is the unconscious musical lilt of English spoken by the local people. Conversations, even at the most mundane or even boring levels, were always a great pleasure to hear even if one did not choose to listen to them.

For the first time in my life I found myself living close to mountains but only walked once in the Brecon Beacons and that was on a very wet day. Perhaps the weather had dampened my mood, because these mountains seemed to be unattractive great lumps, totally without charm. In addition to a thorough soaking I also failed to find any suitable paths. With a very busy lifestyle, there never seemed to be enough time to seek out those who went hill walking in South Wales. On the other hand I never encountered anyone who was remotely interested in it either.

However, a nearby area proved a great boon for all the family. We lived on the west side of Swansea, close to the diverse scenery of the Gower Peninsula. Its prominent central hills, of only modest height, were mostly covered by open moorland. These were of ancient sandstone, similar to that of Exmoor, only a short distance away across the Bristol Channel. In sharp contrast, southern Gower was composed of white mountain limestone which immediately brought back memories of my earlier Derbyshire rambles. This rock was particularly evident in the crags overlooking the valley leading down from Bishopston, almost a Derbyshire Dale, and along the whole length of Gower's south coast from the Mumbles to Worms Head, apart from breaks at broad sandy bays. Northwards, Gower's hills dropped down to the marshes of the Loughor Inlet and the broad Whitford Sands. However, the Gower scene was at its most striking in the extreme west, where prominent Rhossili Down provided a backdrop to the long serpentine Worms Head.

This peninsula represented, albeit on a very small scale, some of the very best scenery I had previously encountered in England. Indeed the analogy to England went much further, because many of the place names on Gower, particularly those in the south, were of Anglo-Saxon origin, such as Horton, Oxwich, Langland and Caswell. I also read somewhere that the local dialect was once akin to a West Country burr, but by the time I came to know the area the singsong of Swansea had definitely taken over. My family have a keen interest in traditional folk music and I was fascinated to learn about Phil Tanner who was born on Gower, and lived there until his death in 1950, never having left it once in a long lifetime. Yet he had a repertoire of over one hundred local folk songs in the English language. This part of Wales once had strong ties with England because Somerset is close by and until recent times numerous small trading vessels carried a wide variety of cargoes to and fro across the Bristol Channel. While connections between the two communities had once been even stronger, I still felt very much at home in this particular 'Little England beyond Wales'.

Family summer holidays were spent camping in West Wales and we became familiar with the coast from the Gower all the way up to Barmouth, with Pembrokeshire our favourite. Our numerous short walks were limited by the capability of Matthew the youngest family member and his most striking early achievement was in climbing up to Llyn Cau on Cader Idris when only three years old. Unsurprisingly, he has been a very active mountain walker ever since.

My own energetic walking recommenced when I left home on fine summer days to stride along the south coast of Gower to join the rest of my family who had come out by car and were already ensconced on the beaches at either Horton or Port Eynon. However, my most memorable walk during this period took place when the other family members were away visiting our parents in Nottingham. It was a weekend and, as the weather on the Saturday turned out to be fine and warm, I decided to take a long walk around the high points of Gower before returning along its southern coast. Leaving my car behind at Penmaen, I set out across the length of Cefn Bryn, a moorland sandstone ridge which extends across the centre of Gower. Ryer's Down, the pretty little village of Cheriton and then Llanmadoc Hill followed. From the last there were extensive views of the burrows and sandy beach reaching out into the Loughor Inlet behind Gower.

By now it was clear that I was heading for trouble. My former walking boots had been thrown away after debased use during the construction of our new home's garden and had not been replaced. So, on this day, I was wearing new cheap gardening boots which did not fit properly and were already painful. The discomfort worsened and so did the blisters associated with it. On reaching the top of Rhossili Down I was obliged to remove these offending articles to allow a temporary respite for my suffering feet.

On this warm sunny day there could not have been a better place to stop, rest and contemplate. One of the nearby old burial chambers on this high, exposed place was said to mark Sweyne's tomb, although archaeological evidence suggested that these tumuli had been here long before he came to these parts. Sweyne, a Nordic chieftain, was reputed to have been the founder of Swansea, originally Sweyne's Isle, a former fortified islet at the mouth of the River Tawe. Whether true or not, the summit of Rhossili Down could not have been bettered for his final resting place. Far below the lovely golden sands of Rhossili Bay, stretched in a gentle curve all the way from the rocks at Burry Holms to those at Worms Head, disturbed at only one spot where the bare wooden ribs of an old sailing vessel still emerged from below their surface. Beyond these a blue sea led out towards the broad Atlantic, the way that Sweyne and his companions would have first come in their long boats. The long humped serpentine shape of Worms Head, with its near-side in dark shadow in the middle of that sunny day, provided the most compulsive attraction for the eye in a broad scene extending far away to distant shining water. The name of this headland might seem unusual, but is appropriate for this long, thin, rugged and curvaceous peninsula, because 'Worm' means 'Serpent' in Old English.

Most reluctantly I replaced my boots and made my way down to Rhossili before continuing along the combe to Mewslade Bay and the limestone coast on the south side of Gower. The path now followed the ups and downs and ins and outs of a beautiful stretch of south-facing coast composed of white rocks and cliffs. Ancient settlements had been sited on the tops above and caves in the cliffs beneath had once provided a home for Stone Age man. But these did not attract my attention on that day because the pain of my blistered feet now dominated my world. Wonderful, but only temporary, relief came on reaching Port Eynon Bay. Here, masquerading as an enthusiastic paddler, I walked along the soft sand with my bare feet immersed in soothing salt water, passing others enjoying a fine summer's day on the beach. Then after a miserable climb over Oxwich Point, I was again able to return to the sand and salt water treatment for the long length of Oxwich Bay. Without these periodic respites, I do not think that I could have reached my car on foot. For the final climb I did not attempt to put my boots back on again because that operation alone would have been far too painful. So, in the company of families leaving for home after a happy day on the beach, I climbed barefoot up the sand, stones and dried mud back to my car, all the while attempting to disguise my acute discomfort from those around me.

That evening, after my sorry feet had responded to medication, I was able to sit back and ponder, not on the pain that had been, but on the special enjoyment the day had given me. I have remembered it since with great pleasure because it marks the key point in my life when I returned to serious walking after an absence of ten years.

By the beginning of 1966 we were again on the move, first to London and then to the South Bank of the Humber where I would be once again in my home region.

CHAPTER ELEVEN

LINCOLNSHIRE AGAIN

The Lincolnshire to which I returned in 1968 was very different from the county I had left twenty years before. For one thing, my new base in the northern part of the county was in an unknown area and, for another, the countryside and to a lesser extent the towns had become affluent in the interim. Although Grimsby's fishing industry, on which the fortunes of the modern town had been based, was then in decline, this had been replaced by a host of new ones based on food processing, oil and chemicals. This new industrial belt extended upstream to Immingham and beyond, but not into the rural hinterland.

Away from the drained sea marshes beside the Humber Estuary and the North Sea shore, the ground rose towards the rolling chalk upland of the Lincolnshire Wolds, the hills that had been visible along the western skyline during my childhood at Chapel St. Leonards. They form part of the extensive chalk uplands centred on Salisbury Plain which extend up here through the Chilterns and the East Anglian hills with a break at the Wash.

We chose to live in Caistor, a small town on the site of an ancient settlement, later fortified by the Romans. Standing on a hill spur projecting from the western scarp of the Wolds and overlooking the broad Ancholme valley, it was a quaint, even quixotic place, which in more fashionable Southern England, would by then have become a smart tourist attraction. However, located in an isolated and relatively unknown corner of England, it had remained an unpretentious workaday place. Our new home was some ten miles away over the top of the Wolds from my workplace on the Humber Bank.

Changes to farming and the countryside scene were most striking. Farm mechanisation, already underway when I left two decades before, had now been carried through to completion. This and the monoculture that came with it had led to the loss of most hedges and trees in order to maximise crop production and to provide better access for new much larger farm equipment. Another striking outcome of these changes was the drastic reduction in numbers of farm workers. To my regret this loss of rural population also meant that nearly all the local public footpaths, except for a few in the immediate vicinity of the larger settlements, had now become disused. The extent of this rural change is demonstrated by the fact that, when my Grandfather was a young farm labourer in the second half of the nineteenth century, the large Wolds farms had employed up to thirty men and more than that number of horses. By the late 1960s there were no horses and probably only two workers at most.

For the first three years following my return, the pressure of work allowed little time for walking except on Sunday mornings and then I found myself plodding along nearby country roads. These were of two types, the few ancient ones which wandered along in delightful fashion and the majority which were straight and had mostly been laid out during the land enclosures of the preceding century. In that virtually treeless scene of large fields, empty and bleak in winter and covered by single crop carpets in summer, there were few birds in the air and very little wildlife on the ground. The best that can be said about those Sunday morning walks was that there was hardly any traffic, the air was fresh and cool and that they provided good exercise.

From study of local Ordnance Survey maps it was possible to deduce where footpaths might once have existed when the rural population had been higher. The presumed routes mostly linked villages or led to parish churches. I also assumed that the old country folk, who had been obliged to go everywhere on foot, would also have chosen the most convenient routes. From this analysis I came up with three possible footpaths in the vicinity of Caistor. These observations were set down in a letter which I then sent to the local council, politely asking for advice on their possible legal status. For a long time there was no reply, but when it came the response proved to be a beautiful piece of work summarising the current status of legislation on public rights of way, of which I was well aware, but did not contain even a passing reference to my request for information on the three possible footpaths. At that, and probably as intended by the official who penned it, I gave the matter up as a bad job. But only temporarily until I had more time to devote to the subject.

During this road walking period, I discovered that the present day lonely emptiness of the Wolds had not always been thus. In fact the region had once been one of the most heavily farmed and populated parts of England. From the first Neolithic farmers onwards, waves of settlers, many from across the North Sea, had arrived here, settled and worked the land. Unfortunately, very little of their handiwork had survived down to modern times apart from the ancient High and Bluestone Heath Streets, which ran along the length of these hills, and a few Bronze Age and Iron Age burial mounds that had not been ploughed out. However, the most obvious survival from the past was the plethora of Danish place names left by a late wave of settlers. Some of these applied to present day villages, and others to former villages now reduced to single farms. This area became the heartland of the Danelaw following the settlement of Danish farmers and their families a thousand years before. The population was subsequently decimated by the plagues of the Middle Ages, culminating in the Black Death, and, although sheep farming later became prosperous, the human population never recovered. From my walks it soon became patently obvious that there were now far fewer people up here on these lonely hills than there had been for many centuries.

Although my initial local walking efforts had not been successful, there were compensations for being in this part of the country. For although Lincolnshire is a part of Lowland England, it is one which lies well to the north. For instance our home town of Caistor, which never considered itself to be in Northern England, was both further north than Sheffield and at the same latitude as Manchester. Here the North was regarded as beginning at Yorkshire which, in spite of close historic and linguistic affiliations, was locally regarded as an alien region, a prejudice dating back to Anglo-Saxon times when Yorkshire had been part of powerful Northumbria and Lincolnshire part of equally powerful Mercia.

Thus the Peak District, the South Pennines, the Yorkshire Dales, the North Yorkshire Moors and even Northumberland and the Lake District were not far away and we took every advantage of their proximity at weekends and holiday times. The first and last of these were the most visited because they had been my first great upland loves and at the same time represented two very different epitomes of wild countryside beauty. It gave me great delight to introduce my children to the pleasures of these regions at an early age, and I am happy to say that all have remained keen hill and mountain walkers ever since.

The Peak District was a convenient distance from our home for day trips and the area which included Kinder Scout, Castleton, the Winnats, Mam Tor, Lose Hill and Win Hill became a great favourite. I also found Kinder Scout a wonderful place to calm the soul and put life into its proper perspective after particularly hectic periods at work. We climbed up from Edale on many occasions, from times when the frozen peat on the top was deep in snow and when wind borne water from the Downfall flew back up to form massive icicles dangling from all nearby rock surfaces, to the other extreme, when, after long dry periods, this typically wet desert could become a strange parched one and then the wind carried roaming clouds of dust across the plateau.

Our most memorable day trip to Kinder at this period was with my eldest son's French exchange student. His home was in rural France far from hills and the only part of England he had seen so far was our area and views from the bus on the way up from the South Coast. With this in mind we thought it might be a good idea to show him a rather different part of our country before he returned to France, and Kinder Scout seemed an appropriate contrast. At the outset I should mention that we had a communication problem. Our French was poor and his English not good and furthermore it had failed to improve during his stay because the French children had persistently remained together as a compact group. Our visitor, insofar as he understood what our proposed trip was about, seemed happy to come along with us. However, when he saw us collecting our rucksacks, rain gear and boots and making similar provision for him, his face wore an expression which can only be described as one of wry amusement. It crossed my mind that he might have thought that it was both customary and fashionable for the English to wear fancy clothing on days out in the countryside.

We all climbed into our family car and headed west first through gently rolling farming country, then across the flat plain of the River Trent and finally into the undulating coal mining and industrial region of North

Nottinghamshire/South Yorkshire. Up to this point our visitor viewed the passing scene with limited interest, but when we encountered the first stretch of heather covered moorland close to Sheffield, his expression became one of surprise. Unfortunately, the weather was deteriorating and his eyes opened even wider on seeing the cloud covered tops around Edale, the starting point for our walk. During the subsequent climb up Grindsbrook's rocky gully both mist and rain increased. By this time the poor lad had become alarmed and our attempts to reassure him met with only limited success. Then on reaching the gorgeous stark plateau top, as on many previous occasions, we headed off on a compass bearing across the bleak, mist-enshrouded, deep, dark peaty groughs. It may have been a familiar scene to us but for him it was something out of this world.

In view of our visitor's obvious fear, we decided to minimise the length of time on the top by heading straight for Jacobs Ladder rather than detouring to the Downfall as originally intended. Every few yards or so the poor lad exclaimed "How far is eet?" in a plaintive tone, the 'it' presumably being the end of his terror. As nobody else in our party was showing similar fear, it has since crossed my mind that he might have thought that he had been brought to this dreadful place by a group of foreign lunatics.

When the swirling mist and rain revealed a solitary figure looming out of the gloom, the French lad, his English completely abandoning him at this moment of relief, could only exclaim "Un homme". Then he stood by utterly flabbergasted as we only passed the time of day with our fellow walker before going our separate ways. From this point onwards we heard no more from our visitor as he trudged along at the rear of our small group all the way down into Edale. I cannot begin to imagine what he said about this event to his family when he returned home.

With cousin Jean on Chapel Beach in 1934. Note the long gone Sand Hills at the rear.

Denis and Piet on the heathery North Yorkshire Moors in 1950.

Grindsbrook. A very popular access route to the Kinder Plateau.

With the Nottingham Curlews in Monsal Dale, Christmas 1950. Left to right, Peter, Bill, Ernie (1), self, Alan, Ernie (2) and Bill's son inlaw.

My London walking friends on an Ockley Ramble. Novenber 1950.

The Yorkshire Dales. Wandering over the tops from Muker to Askrigg in 1950.

The South West. Outside the Luttrell Arms, Dunster in 1951.

An alfresco lunch with Norman on the Cornish cliffs. Note the ubiquitous tin plate meths cooker.

The Yorkshire Dales. Gaping Ghyll in 1951.

The Shropshire hills in 1952. Caer Carodoc from the Long Mynd.

The Western Highlands in 1952. Where Barrisdale meets Loch Hourn.

The Lakes. Pavey Ark from Blea Rigg on a snowy bright January day in 1954.

With Sunya, a very special girl friend, in North Wales. Summer 1954.

Rhossili Bay, Gower.

With Sooty, a faithfull family friend on the Lakeland Fells in 1970.

Exmoor 1979. Back after thirty years absence.

Tarr Steps across Exmoor's River Barle.

Sunya in the Lake District in the early 1980's.

A favourite spot in the Chilterns. Footbridge over the River Chess.

Sunya and Flissie on Exmoor in the 1980's.

The Somerset Coast from the high moorland near Selworthy Beacon.

Sunya approaching Musala Hut, Bulgaria on the way up to the summit.

The lonely emptiness of the Lincolnshire Coast. Spring 1992.

The only other living creatures on the long Delph Bank leading up to Lincoln.

The all but abandoned straight Ermine Street south of Lincoln.

Exton, Rutland. The most beautiful village by far on the way across England.

On the Cotswold Way approaching Bath.

The end of the 536 miles journey across England.

With Sunya on Loughrigg Fell, the Lake District, in autumn 2003.

Tranquil Grasmere in the Lake District, Autumn 2003.

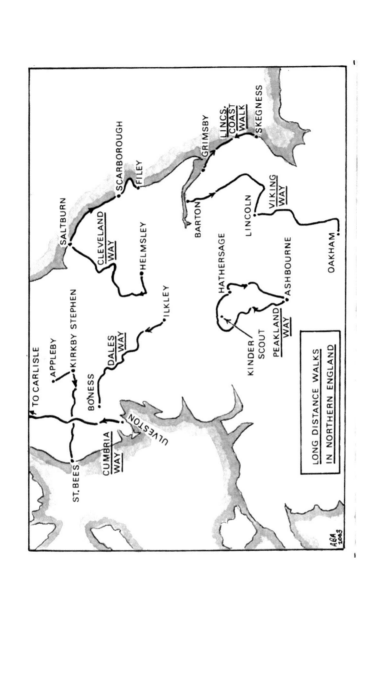

LONG DISTANCE WALKS
IN NORTHERN ENGLAND

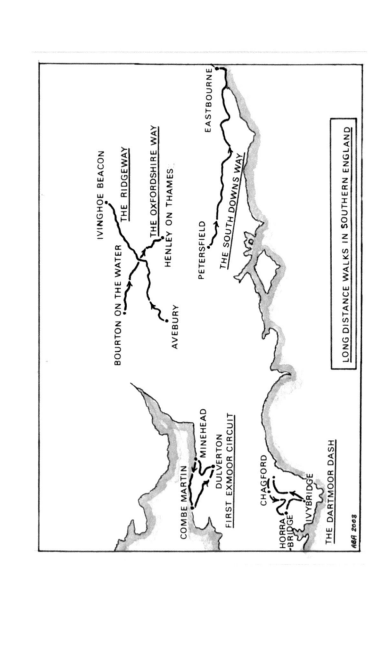

LONG DISTANCE WALKS IN SOUTHERN ENGLAND

IVINGHOE BEACON
THE RIDGEWAY
BOURTON ON THE WATER
THE OXFORDSHIRE WAY
HENLEY ON THAMES
AVEBURY

PETERSFIELD
THE SOUTH DOWNS WAY
EASTBOURNE

COMBE MARTIN
MINEHEAD
DULVERTON
FIRST EXMOOR CIRCUIT

CHAGFORD
HORRA BRIDGE
IVYBRIDGE
THE DARTMOOR DASH

ABA 2008

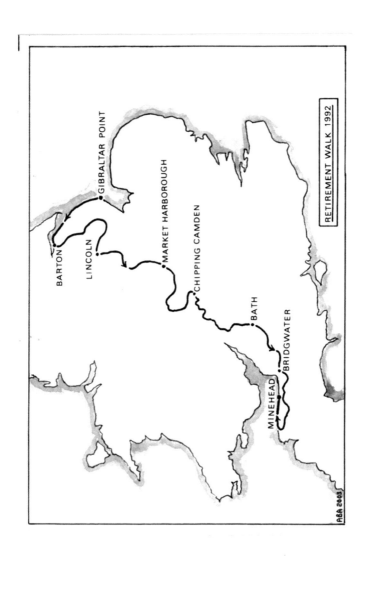

RETIREMENT WALK 1992

BARTON

GIBRALTAR POINT

LINCOLN

MARKET HARBOROUGH

CHIPPING CAMDEN

BATH

BRIDGWATER

MINEHEAD

RBA 2003

CHAPTER TWELVE

NEV

Strict chronological order was not followed in the last chapter because I wished to give my old friend Nev and 'The Wanderlust' one of their own.

Returning to the problem of finding public footpaths in the Lincolnshire Wolds, as my request for information from the local authority had been unsuccessful, I then followed the proven route which had been successful for both the Weald and the Peak District many years before. That was to seek out experienced local walkers. The search initially proved fruitless and then someone suggested that a certain Nev Cole might be the man I was looking for. I wrote to him, stating that my family and I had recently arrived in North Lincolnshire and that we were interested in joining his rambling club. I received a courteous reply with an offer of help with transport, but unfortunately this missive coincided with unexpectedly heavy demands from work and for many months I had no opportunity of rambling.

We did eventually meet one evening in 1970 at Caistor Grammar School where he had come to give a slide show to the pupils and I tagged along with my eldest son. He proved to be a rather small man in his late fifties with a sharp-featured, sensitive face and the stamp of the countryman about him. The last was particularly evident in his soft Lincolnshire accent and his slow but deliberate actions. His talk that night was on his favourite subject,

'Rambling in Lincolnshire'.

Speaking with gentle enthusiasm in a seemingly unrehearsed manner, his audience soon responded. The slides illustrating his talk had been collected over a long period and ranged from the big skies and broad acres of the region to its many intimate corners and architectural delights. Underlying all was wistfulness for things past, for the buildings which had been abandoned and demolished and for a countryside that had changed so much in recent times. As I already shared the same views, it gave me pleasure to at last meet a man after my own heart. That meeting was the start of a treasured friendship.

It was appropriate that we met in Caistor because Nev was attached to the small town. Although brought up in Cleethorpes, his family origins were here and as a youngster he grew to love the surrounding countryside during school holidays spent at his grandmother's home. Nearby, the steep scarp slope of the Wolds was broken into short steep-sided dales which had resisted the incursion of arable farming. Part way down each one, water issued from springs to run as clear becks over sandstone pebbles. This was the scene which had nurtured Nev's lifelong love for the Lincolnshire countryside.

Over a period I gradually discovered the history of rambling in this part of the world. The inter-war years had seen the birth of the first great outdoor movement all over the country. At a time of harsh economic hardship, many town dwellers turned to the countryside of their ancestors for escape and recreation. The industrial towns, which had always been unattractive, must have been particularly bleak at this period and one of these was the Grimsby/Cleethorpes conurbation. However, open countryside was only a short step away and this included both unchanged and reclaimed sea marshes, and inland there were the chalk hills of the Lincolnshire Wolds. The gentle slopes of the last rolled up to a chalk plateau broken by many secret and wandering valleys which were their true delight.

These were the scenes that attracted youngsters of the inter-war years. They came in clubs of different origins, ranging from chapel congregations to an exotic-sounding Esperanto Rambling Club. Now all but forgotten, Esperanto was an invented international language which enjoyed a short popularity at the time. One of these local clubs was founded by a young Nev in 1932 and all the members were lads and lassies in their teens. The name they chose, 'The Wanderlust Rambling Club', might now seem rather trite but it encapsulated the romanticism and youthful vigour of its first members.

Much of Lincolnshire is good farmland, but by the 1930s the farming industry was in serious decline. With cheap food available from abroad and no farming subsidies, whole areas of the countryside now had a neglected appearance, with much arable land becoming pasture or even reverting to waste. Fortunately, the network of once well trodden countryside footpaths and tracks still existed. Forty years later I gained an excellent insight to the period through the Wanderlust Logs, a series of dog-eared notebooks which were the club's most treasured possession. These contained details of rambles, embellished where appropriate with press cuttings and photos. The club cycled out from town to the ramble venues, so cycle capes were worn for rain protection when both cycling and walking. In addition, the lads wore long woollen stockings and voluminous shorts topped by sports jackets. However, photos showed the girls in everyday clothes apart from the heavy hob nailed boots which all wore. As befits growing youngsters there were frequent references to food, 'mountains' of which were brought from home, and to the great tuck-ins at tea shops, most of which have long since disappeared.

Time can lend a halcyon image to the past, but in the background there were serious concerns which had an impact on those rambles. So, in addition to walk descriptions, the Logs also referred to animated discussions on Mussolini's brutal invasion of Abyssinia and the likely effects of modern aerial warfare. The Second World War was on its way.

Nev was in the army for five years, seeing action in France, the Western Desert, Sicily and Italy. He said little to me about his wartime experiences, only once intimating that the long separation from his young wife had been a lifetime regret. He had married one of his club members shortly before the war, and by the time I met him he was a widower.

When the club re-formed in 1945, it was a more mature group in a countryside which had changed dramatically in response to the desperate wartime need to grow more food. Most of the pasture had been converted to arable land and many of the former beautiful green lanes and paths had been obliterated, a trend which sadly continued long after the immediate post war period. Farm mechanisation also led to less jobs and therefore there were fewer country people around to walk the paths. As village populations declined, shops, pubs and schools closed and public transport withered away. These changes took place all over lowland England but nowhere have their effects been more marked than on the rich, but nowadays very lonely, farmland of Lincolnshire.

With the radical changes to the countryside and the new attitude of society at large, it is not surprising that post war rambling did not regain its former popularity. There were now very few local walking clubs, but the Wanderlust prospered for a while under Nev's guiding hand. One lady who had been an active member of the club in the 1960s once told me that there had been too little wander and too much lust in her time! I believe she was referring to a record number of club marriages at that period.

Belatedly, new footpath legislation appeared in the 1960s with the creation of a national definitive footpath system. Nev gladly dedicated much of his precious spare time to give evidence at official footpath enquiries, attempting to protect them wherever possible. During this period the Club Logs of the 1930s were used more than once as evidence of footpath use but although some battles were won, regrettably, many more were lost.

Things were at a low ebb when we took up rambling in Lincolnshire. Sometimes our small family group accounted for the majority of those present on rambles and the Wanderlust were now the only active group over a wide area. At the time it seemed as though the prosperous and increasingly materialistic urban society around us had irrevocably turned its back on countryside walking.

In these circumstances it is not surprising that walking in the Lincolnshire countryside was now very difficult. The old footpath system had been all but destroyed and often the only tracks which remained were those currently used by farmers. Any evidence on the ground of paths, which in theory still existed, was often hard to find because stiles had frequently been removed and signposts were virtually non-existent. My earlier frustrated effort to get information from the local authority turned out to be the norm.

As a native of the county I felt that I had more right to these wide open spaces than the limited view obtained from the verges of increasingly busy roads, and despaired at times because few held similar views. Then I met Nev and from that time onwards he was always there to proffer advice and encouragement. Although he rarely showed his own feelings, I came to appreciate them. He had lost his much loved wife a few years before and then the firm where he had worked and advanced since youth was bought out and shut down. However, I can only remember one occasion when his feelings actually got the better of him and that was on a wet and misty day at the beginning of a year. Our small party had been following a compass bearing on a sticky slow tramp along the theoretical line of a public footpath across a vast newly ploughed muddy prairie. After a while we came to a small dip in the ground which we at first failed to identify. Then Nev suddenly remembered it as the site of a coppice and hedgerow which had been full of wild flowers and bird life the last time he was here. With uncharacteristic deep despair he went on to say that it would only be a matter of time before all footpaths in Lincolnshire would be like this one.

At the time none of us imagined that change was coming. The first sign was an increase in enquiries about the club and this was followed by an explosion in numbers coming out on rambles. Within eighteen months the club was prospering to an extent that had not been known since the 1930s. The first great outdoor movement had given birth to the Wanderlust and now forty years later the second was transforming it. This first one had provided an escape from the drab towns of the Depression years and the second from realisation that personal materialism, which had been the driving force of society since the Second World War, was not the be all and end all of life.

The new membership was different from that of the 1930s, because it now consisted of family groups and the middle-aged. It was also apparent that many who now joined the club had not originally intended to do so. With a new desire to walk in the countryside, they had been thwarted by a lack of sign posting, destroyed paths, misleading notices and sometimes unfriendly receptions.

In these circumstances many turned to the only walking club still active in the Grimsby area and, having joined, usually stayed on as people of like interests united in comradeship.

The rapid increase in numbers brought its own problems. One of these was space for car parking at walk venues and another the shortage of leaders to meet the demands of an expanded ramble programme. Although the change was gratifying, almost overnight we had switched from lonely walks to being members of a small army moving across the countryside, something which was not to my liking. When leading I usually asked Nev to be the tail ender, not only because I knew that he would do an excellent job, but also because his bald head was visible at a distance!

The situation improved as new members gained confidence in leading. The County Council also began installing footpath signs, although many of these did not stay upright or even survive for very long. However, the greatest step forward came with the new 1:50,000 Ordnance Survey maps which, for the first time, depicted public rights of way. Unfortunately, the number of public footpaths in our locality turned out to be disappointingly few. Around this time a former rare experience became a regular occurrence. We were meeting other ramblers on our walks.

Throughout this flurry of activity, Nev's measured approach to the club's management remained unchanged in a manner that would have put many senior industrialists of my acquaintance to shame. He always handled meetings in a constructive and courteous manner, especially when it was necessary to steer ladies away from animated irrelevant chatter. It is now nearly a quarter of a century since my wife and I left the Wanderlust Rambling Club, but from time to time we hear that it is still doing well.

One of the high points of Nev's life took place in the autumn of 1976 and this was the opening of the Viking Way. He and I walked along the provisional route from Grantham to Tealby, a pretty village on the western edge of the Wolds, where the official opening ceremony took place. We covered the eighty miles in three and a half days and had a great time marching across the Vale of Belvoir, along the Lincoln Cliff, over a small section of Fenland not far from Lincoln and finally over the Wolds. At that early stage the Way did not pass through Lincoln as it does today.

In Lincolnshire's lonely countryside we met very few people along the way but our quiet companionship was more than enough. Often neither of us spoke for hours on end. Then at Donnington-on-Bain we met a group of our friends and continued on with them to join the crowd at the official opening. The terrace in front of Tealby village hall, serving as a platform, was filled to capacity with Lincolnshire's great and good, many of whom I did not know. As the secretary of the Lincolnshire Area of the Ramblers' Association for many years, Nev had worked tirelessly to bring the Way into being. It was typical of the man that on this special day he had to be coerced to take his rightful place on the platform.

With the club's increasing success, we became more ambitious and made coach trips to the nearby Peak and the South Pennines which, to be frank, had always attracted me far more than the Lincolnshire scene. Nev came with us on these occasions and while he enjoyed himself and never said anything to the contrary, I was always left with the impression that he found this beautiful rugged countryside in some way wanting compared to his own special Lincolnshire.

I was transferred from Lincolnshire to London in 1978 and from that time onwards did not see him as often as I would have liked. Our last meeting came towards the end. By then he looked frail but at heart was still his old enthusiastic self. Then in death I learnt something about him that I had never known in life. While in the army during the war he had been awarded the MBE for gallantry. It was typical of the man.

I often think of the times spent in the lonely open countryside of my native county, and when these thoughts turn to the gentle rolling Wolds, I am always reminded of one of nature's true gentlemen who gained so much enjoyment from wandering along its quiet ways. In spirit I am sure he does so still.

CHAPTER THIRTEEN

SOME LOCAL WALKS

For a decade I explored the length and breadth of north Lincolnshire and got to know it well. Much of its agriculture was intensive, often a monoculture where crop growth depended on the liberal application of chemical fertilisers, herbicides and weed killers. I never felt comfortable in these surroundings because to my mind the practise represented land use verging on abuse. There were two visually dominant effects, but not necessarily the ones representing the greatest damage. The first was the unnatural, almost purple hue, of growing cereals brought about by the overgenerous application of nitrogen rich fertilisers. The second took the form of numerous white scars on the slopes of the Wolds where the thin top soil had been lost through a combination of deep ploughing and subsequent erosion by the elements. In these latter places crops did manage to grow but were sub-standard and totally dependent on chemicals added by man.

A lifetime's intimate contact with the countryside has shown me that there has to be both give and take in all our dealings with nature and that if a balance is not maintained the result can be a sorry mess. Taken to its extreme, when man attacks nature, nature will ultimately hit back in unpleasant and unexpected ways which will always be to man's detriment. These were not comfortable thoughts to have in one's mind while wandering through the countryside for pleasure, but in Lincolnshire it was rarely possible to escape from them.

However, two scenes not far from our Caistor home were very different. The first of these was the extensive woodland to the north and east of Market Rasen. Below the scarp slope of the Wolds there was a belt of sandy soil where agriculture would have always been difficult. I do not know for certain, but visual evidence, mostly in the form of tree ages and the condition and type of abandoned farm buildings, suggested that the forest near Market Rasen had been created from abandoned farms during the lean inter-war agricultural period. There was a pleasing range of tree types to suit the varying dry and wet terrains and, most important of all, these woods were managed by the Forestry Commission and therefore open to the public. I found them a wonderful place of escape when tired of the large open fields all around.

One feature in this remote woodland had a special place in our national history. A small but prominent tree covered rise in these woods, known as Hambleton Hill, is believed to have been the spot where a large army of peasants and local gentry had once camped overnight. They were the initial wave of the widespread revolt which later became known by the resounding title of the Pilgrimage of Grace. Next day they marched on to Lincoln with great expectations, but on arrival only found lack of leadership and deceit. The terrible wrath of King Henry VIII was to visit them later. Religion was then a key part of everyday life and the insurgents had become increasingly alarmed by the changes which the king was making to their church, including the dissolution of many religious houses, the commandeering of their buildings and land, the acquisition by the Crown of many church treasures and the major reduction of Saints' days in the church calendar. So widespread was the disturbance that for a time the King completely lost control of the whole of the north of England.

While the woodlands around Rasen were open to the general public, other equally attractive ones on the Wolds to the north of Caistor were not. These extended in a great curving swath across the gentle northern slopes of the Wolds before dropping down to the ancestral home of a noble lord. All this land and much more beside had once belonged to nearby Thornton Abbey. After the religious dissolution I believe these parts came into the possession of his family in return for services rendered to the Tudor monarchy. Within these trees, extending over high ground and intervening valleys, there were appealing broad grassy rides. Present day Lincolnshire is noted for the paucity of its public footpaths. This situation was at its most extreme here, for over a wide area, including these woodlands, there were hardly any at all.

It seemed a shame that these nearby delectable woods should be totally closed to walkers, so I decided to enquire whether it might be possible to lead a rambling party through them on a date convenient to the owner. My point of contact was the lord's agent whom, I noted, although an obvious civilian, still retained a modest army officer rank. I phoned this gentleman and very politely asked him for the permission which I sought. There was a distinct pause before the reply and when it came it was in clipped very precise upper class English.

'We really cannot do with you people.'

Another long pause followed during which I mistakenly thought that he might be relenting. But the follow up when it came was most patronising.

'Don't y'know that there is a perfectly good public highway which passes through the vicinity.'

At that point all my plebeian ire was roused. I very nearly said something that would have wrecked any future hope of gaining permission to enter these woods, but fortunately just managed to keep myself in check. In part, my reaction was due to familiarity with the road, which was on my daily route to and from work. Running long and straight it passed through these woods in two places but only for very short distances.

I do not know whether the situation has improved today, but maybe it was beginning to change even then, because when I next resolved to seek permission for our club a year or so later it was granted without demur.

News that a rare walk was about to take place through these private woodlands must have spread far and wide because on the warm sunny day in question a large crowd, mostly of people unknown to me, including a party of foreign visitors, arrived at the starting point in Caistor Market Place. As no restriction had been placed on the number in the party, I decided, with some misgiving, to allow all of them to come along. Nev was at the tail and he counted ninety-four participants as they wound their way out of the square! Thank goodness I have never since had responsibility for a similar large number on a walk. Two miles along the way it became apparent that we had acquired yet another participant. She was an extremely large goat who, in friendly fashion, had decided to leave her home patch to join in the day's most unusual fun. The number on the walk then reduced to ninety-three when Tom Richards, a local parish councillor, took hold of the goat's halter, which fortunately was still attached, and led her back home. From that point onwards the walk proceeded without mishap. As the invading army moved through the normally forbidden sunny glades, I looked out for signs of the lord's minions. None were visible but we could have been kept under observation from a distance.

Without doubt my favourite Lincolnshire scene harked back to my early days on the coast. Chapel St. Leonards, with its Sand Hills now gone and extensive new building developments, may have become a poor imitation of its former self, but many miles of unspoilt coast still remain. For me this attraction evolved into a mini long distance walk along the shore between Skegness and Cleethorpes.

Depending on the immediate coastal scene, the sea could be judged to be either aggressive or benign. After the railway arrived at the former hamlet of Skegness in the latter half of the nineteenth century, it rapidly developed into a full blown seaside resort with an imposing esplanade. From that time onwards and until recently, the sea decided to move away and the previous foreshore grew so broad that in the course of time it acquired gardens, a boating lake and amusement parks. However, only a short distance to the north the sea has always threatened, with the flat land behind now protected by a substantial concrete sea wall which extends to Chapel St. Leonards. The inland scene here was no better, for beyond the pleasant buildings of Skegness there were seemingly endless holiday camps, caravan sites and amusement arcades. While walking past these it was preferable to keep one's gaze permanently averted towards the sea. Then beyond Chapel a lovely lonely section of coast composed of sea, sandy shore and dunes backed by open farmland continued up to the vicinity of Mablethorpe. When the sea next goes on the offensive, as it assuredly will, the exposed coast between Skegness and Mablethorpe can be expected to bear the brunt of any attack.

After Mablethorpe, one of my favourite stretches of coast, with its wide beaches and broad sand dunes, led on to Saltfleet. From here samphire covered sea marsh intervened between the coast and the place where new sand dunes were forming out at the true edge of the water, a sure sign that here the sea was retreating. At Donna Nook, said to have been named after a wrecked sailing ship, the coast veered towards the Humber Estuary. Apart from the nearby bombing range, this was a wild lonely place where grey seals often lay in rows on the distant shoreline and foxes were occasionally evident in the broad grassy dunes on the edge of the land. Later, the route followed a man-made embankment with flat farmland on the left and sea marsh on the right as part-formed dunes continued next to the sea. Now my only companions were herons side slipping on the wind between their fishing places in numerous small freshwater ponds on the landward side of the sea wall.

The sandy shore rejoined the land at Humberstone Fitties, with Yorkshire's Spurn Point only a short distance away across a deep water shipping channel. The walk then followed a sea wall along the now broad Humber Estuary. Here, the most striking feature was the boundary between the Earth's Eastern and Western Hemispheres. This was in the form of a permanent line across the bank and a signpost pointing towards some of the earth's more important far off places. On my early trips distant Cleethorpes and Grimsby first took on an exotic appearance, a compound of the golden domes on top of the Winter Gardens at Cleethorpes and the tall Venetian-style hydraulic tower on Grimsby Docks. Nowadays a large far less appealing box-like structure on the sea front at Cleethorpes disrupts this view. Finally, the bustle of Cleethorpes replaced the many quiet shoreline miles.

I know of no other stretch of coast in this country where a similar sandy beach can match it in solitude, length and seemingly infinite surrounding space. Yes, this is the part of Lincolnshire which I undoubtedly love the best.

CHAPTER FOURTEEN

LONG DISTANCES

By the early 1970s long distance paths were becoming popular and these began to attract my attention, especially after the pleasurable forays along the Lincolnshire coast. The idea of progressing many miles through constantly changing scenes held great appeal. Yet in spite of their obvious attractions, long distance walks soon proved to have one common disconcerting characteristic. The end of each, a cherished goal while heading towards it, always brought sudden total deflation on arrival. In this respect I believe each one was only mirroring life because it is the journey which is all important and not the end.

From the outset I decided to dispense with my tent and camping gear although nowadays these are much lighter in weight. The alternative might be more expensive, but there would be proper beds to sleep on at night, meals provided at the beginning and end of each day, the comfort of daily baths, regular changes of clothing and, most important of all, the load on my back was not likely to be more than six kilograms.

My wife was a brick and became a serious countryside walker from the day that she first met me. However, she drew the line at long distance walking, because for her the idea of tramping day after day carrying a bulky rucksack held no appeal. So from the outset it was clear that my long distance walks would either be with others or alone. Until they acquired commitments of their own, one of my two sons almost always came along with me. As my wife would no longer be sharing part of my limited holidays, I decided that my yearly long distance walks, for that is what they became, would be limited to a maximum of eight days, usually taken around Easter time. This arrangement continued for fifteen years. But on retirement I finally had the golden opportunity for a much more ambitious project.

Special walks with my sons began at the time when all the family still holidayed together. Then on an allocated day, Gavin, my eldest son, and I trekked off on our own. He proved a stoic, with never a demur even when unwell. The most memorable of these walks was on Arran when Gavin was still in his mid-teens. We had come here because this was the most accessible Scottish Highland Island from our North Lincolnshire home. Unfortunately, the weather remained poor throughout our stay, being consistently dull and very wet. So on the special day I gave up the idea of climbing craggy Goat Fell for what seemed a far less demanding lower level route. Although the high peaks of Arran are clustered together in the north of the island, the map showed that two valleys in their midst, Glen Iorsa and Gleann Easan Biorach, met at a saddle only 1200 feet above sea level. This projected route would take us from Dougrie on the west coast of the island to Lochranza in the north.

Heavy rain had been falling all night and was still pouring down as we said goodbye to the rest of the family. Dougrie Lodge had an abandoned neglected air, in keeping with the mood of the weather. In addition to myself and my son, our much loved family mongrel, Sooty, came with us, attached to the end of a length of rope for security. Leaving the coast behind we headed north eastwards up the valley, disturbing a large herd of Highland deer not far from the lodge. These proved to be the last signs of life for several hours. A neglected track led up to a small lake and then petered out. As the valley veered northwards, the surrounding scene became very wild, with bare cloud shrouded mountains on all sides. Still the rain poured down.

Our progress was difficult and slow across intermittently boggy and stony ground, but the major problem came from running water. Iorsa Water, although running very full, was not a problem because it was parallel to our route, but side streams tumbling down the adjacent tall mountain side could not be avoided. In better weather these might have been attractive small cascades, but now they were torrents. I enjoy overcoming nature's physical challenges, but one exceptional side stream had a formidable volume as well as a stony bed which was slowly rolling downwards. One moment all was going well and on the next I was prostrate in the water watching poor Sooty being carried away downstream. From this prone position the thought flashed through my mind that this might finally be the day when rescuers would have to come looking for us. Then I saw that the knot on the looped end of Sooty's rope had become trapped between boulders and this had stopped her descent. Apart from being terrified, she seemed unhurt. The only lasting damage became apparent when I struggled up to a standing position and my corduroy trousers descended to my knees. My elasticated braces had failed to cope with the impact and had snapped, a problem that was soon temporarily solved by borrowing a length of cord from my rucksack.

After this the water god, having devised a major test, now gave us some respite and we carried on without further problems up to the saddle. There we discovered a unique phenomenon. Streams were issuing simultaneously in opposite directions from both ends of a substantial lochan located in the saddle, one back towards Dougrie and the other to Lochranza. From here a recognisable path soon led us down into the depths of the next glen and on to Lochranza which, in spite of lessening rain, had a foreboding appearance, heightened by its bleak castle beside the sea. But at least this was civilisation again after the wild scenes. Best of all was the sight of the three smiling faces of the other half of the family who had come up to meet us.

On returning to the hotel we made a discovery. The lower half of my son's body and his underclothes were now dyed the same plum colour as his trousers. Whether this was due to the quality of the dye or that of the water with which he had been liberally wetted, or a combination of both, I do not know.

The first long distance walk was with my eldest son, who was then in his late teens. This was along the Cleveland Way, one of several potential routes not far from our North Lincolnshire home.

Easter fell early that year and in addition winter had lingered into spring. As we were going to the North Yorkshire Moors, a notoriously cool part of England, inevitably the walk was a chilly one. However, the weather remained fine, dry and dull throughout. Our way led westwards from the small town of Helmsley to the edge of the Moors before turning north and eventually east high above the Tees Valley. Up here all life had yet to respond to the arrival of spring. The dark winter garb of the heather contrasted with the bright purple carpets of previous visits and a bitter wind from the North Sea met us on reaching Saltburn.

With the passage of time, only notable incidents of that walk remain in clear memory. Years before I had rounded the coast beyond Saltburn to be confronted by belching smoke, flames and fumes from the nearby steelworks at Skinningrove. Now these were shut down and an air of neglect and decay hung over the site. At the time I remember thinking that it would only be a matter of time before this ravaged site, softened by time and nature, would become a fascinating example of industrial archaeology.

The coast towards the south east was mostly new to me. Staithes, nestling deep into cliffs beside a river mouth, confirmed the image seen on old railway posters. At this season few people were around and we escaped from the cold into a cafe for a welcome cup of tea. The wife of an old fisherman was in charge and apart from him and ourselves the place was empty. The old chap's seafaring days were long gone but he was still kitted out in his nautical gear and, what is more, dying to tell us about those times. He opened the conversation by announcing that the day's dank cold weather was like that of the Newfoundland fishing banks, whereupon his wife chased him off to do a job. By the time he returned, we were in the process of tearing ourselves away in order to reach Whitby in good time.

Sometimes on walks there are inexplicable incidents and one occurred on what I now believe were the cliffs in the vicinity of Kettle Ness. To set the scene, the day's weather was cloudy, hazy, dank and very cold. The coast path was wandering through a deserted maze of old mine workings high above the sea. We had not seen anybody for a long time when, suddenly, a tall slim middle aged-lady, in an unusual long plain light brown dress reaching nearly down to her ankles, appeared about thirty paces uphill on our right moving slowly along. At that moment we were speeding towards Whitby with our mealtime deadline in mind. Several minutes later we looked back to see that the lady had moved down onto the path behind us, and, while the distance between us had remained the same, she was still dawdling! The same pattern of constant distance and an apparent slow speed was repeated a number of times until we began to feel uncomfortable at her presence. Finally, on approaching Sandsend and first signs of other humanity, to our relief we found that she had gone. Subsequent enquiries about this curious incident in Whitby predictably bore no fruit.

The final notable memory of that walk was of the cobles on Filey beach. Some of these fishing boats were beached and others were being manoeuvred into and out of the water. Their high pointed bows, said to have been copied from the Viking ships which once came this way, were such marked contrast to their flat bottomed sterns that the combination at first seemed incongruous. In practise this was an ideal design for landing and launching on this exposed North Sea shore.

My next long distance walk was in the company of my youngest son, Matthew, another stoic character apart from times when his stomach was empty, and three walking friends from Lincolnshire. Starting from Appleby in the Eden valley, we wandered along the Eden Way up the valley towards Kirkby Stephen where we planned to join Wainwright's now famous Coast to Coast Path as it headed westwards. Away from the little used paths beside the placid River Eden there were attractive distant hills on each side and ahead stood the bulky mass of Nine Standards Rigg. The cluster of cairns on its summit were clearly visible in that day's bright light, not an occasion when invading Scots could have mistaken them for an English army, as was said to have been their legendary intent.

On the afternoon of the second day we reached a lonely plateau covered with cushioned turf and deep fissured, sometimes grotesque, limestone pavements. Although long abandoned, mans former presence was evident in the form of white stone walls and the remains of ancient settlements. Some distance away a monument marked the spring where Charles II's Scottish army was said to have obtained water and been addressed by its leader on the march to disaster in England in 1651. It is unlikely that anything to match this event has occurred here since that day.

The surrounding hills were now dotted with curious granite boulders deposited by glaciers during the Ice Ages. Some were life size and at a distance could have been mistaken for humans. With nobody in sight for many miles, I first disbelieved my eyes when two of the stones appeared to move. Then they resolved into four Grimsby backpackers, one of whom I knew well. Ray, a big active man, had taken to the great outdoors relatively late in life and had become a most enthusiastic walker. This meeting was not as unique as it might at first seem because, as I have observed more than once before, those who dwell in flat lowland regions often have a particularly strong attachment to high ones. I might add that Ray had also brought some comfort along in the form of a very large bottle of whisky! After our cheery encounter, the emptiness of that wide scene soon enveloped us once more.

After a night in Shap, we entered the Lake District's cloud shrouded Eastern Fells. On Kidsty Pike, the first big Lakeland hill, dazzling white snow drifts filled all ground depressions and remained piled against stone walls, contrasting with the surrounding sombre black peat and the faded yellows of last season's bog grass. Although bitterly cold up here, the magnificent cloud capped mountains in front made it all worthwhile. The path approached the rim of Patterdale Valley, a deep winding glacier-carved trench partly filled by lovely Ullswater, until it had no alternative but to plunge down over the brink all the way to the bright green valley bottom.

Next day's weather was poor, so we forsook the tops

for Grisedale Pass, passing the spot where some RAF colleagues and I had camped for a weekend twenty-five years before. Then the wind gusted against the sides of our old fashioned cotton tents as the rain fell endlessly. We lay inside and read books by candlelight while never a soul came by, only a few feet away from what has now become a busy walking highway.

From Grasmere we went on to Seatoller, all the while admiring the glorious mountains, tarns and lakes along the way. On a fine morning our small group headed over the hills towards a hollow marking upper Ennerdale. On arrival we could see a great forest of conifers spread along the valley floor like an engulfing black carpet and nearby, close to its boundary, there was a single storey stone hut formerly used by shepherds. This was the Black Sail Youth Hostel where I had passed a memorable evening on my first trip to the Lakes.

We joined Ennerdale Water along its southern shore after passing through delicate silver birches just coming into bud. Only a gentle breeze stirred the water surface as the day mellowed into warm late afternoon. This was the forerunner of 1976's blazing hot summer. Finally at Crag Fell, where a steep cliff drops down into the lake, a scramble over a rocky outcrop above the water took us out of the Lakes and into lower country.

The glacier which once carved its way down lovely lonely Ennerdale towards the sea has left a wide U-shaped valley, part lake-filled, with magnificent crags ranging along both sides. It has escaped tourism because no tarmac highway comes this way. Although by no means alone in loving this valley, I have been told by members of the older generation of walkers that they liked it much better when there was no carpet of conifers.

The changed surroundings were underlined in the pub that evening. The talk might have been about cross-country hound racing but the speakers were all industrial workers. From here we passed through pleasant lower countryside to enter an unattractive old industrial region beside the Irish Sea. The walk ended on the bleak partly developed sea front at St. Bees, a spot seemingly far removed from the unspoilt beauty of the fells.

The Dales Way proved the most enjoyable walk of the period. From the edge of a heavily populated urban region, it led across many beautiful hills before arriving on the shore of England's largest lake. There was usually a river beside the way, so the walk also had many advantages of a lowland one. Our small group included my youngest son, Matthew, who was then fourteen.

This springtime was very different from the cold one on the Cleveland Way. Walking enjoyment is usually compounded from three different but mutually dependent factors, the scenery, the weather and the company, and on this occasion all were of the best. Weather rates almost as high as scenery and on this trip it was sunny and warm for much of the way, enhancing a lasting picture of the new vivid green grass beside a River Wharfe tumbling along its white limestone bed. Not far from this water, bluebells bloomed beneath occasional woods, providing blue carpets more dazzling than distant warm seas.

Not far from the start we encountered the Strid where the River Wharfe can become a roaring torrent through a miniature chasm full of rocks sculptured into strange shapes and then dressed by fronds of fern. It is said that anyone who gets into the Strid never gets out again alive, a saying which was belied by a plump lass in a skin suit playing about like a seal in a deep frothy pool. Suddenly realising that she was being observed, this young lady gave us a half conspiratorial, half embarrassed, smile.

The underlying rock of the region later changed to white mountain limestone and at Linton Falls the water had once powered the adjacent old woollen mill. On a narrow iron footbridge above rushing water and rocks we were confronted by a large ferocious-looking boxer dog, who stood his ground and growled menacingly. For a moment the outcome was uncertain and then, confirming the old adage 'he that is most fearsome fears most', the poor creature turned and ran off whimpering. The owner, unnecessarily apologetic, told us that his dog was terrified of people wearing the high packs popular in those days. At the time I wished that confrontations with aggressive bulls could have had a similar outcome.

We spent that night in Grassington, a former farming and mining village and now a tourist centre. I had been here years before with the Curlews. After exploring Ribblesdale, the Three Peaks and Swale Dale, we had returned to the upper reaches of the Wharfe. Unable to find accommodation in Buckden, we hitched a lift on the back of a lorry heading for Grassington. The countryside was deserted until we reached Kilnsey Crag, a large rock face scraped out of the hillside by a passing glacier during the Ice Ages. Here, a lone artist was at work, and for no good reason we gave him a passing cheer. Later, to our acute embarrassment the same man, easel in hand, entered our lodgings. This good mannered professional artist, apart from recognition, made no reference to our earlier unseemly behaviour. Afterwards, we admired his current half-finished painting of Kilnsey Crag, full of realism and bold patterns, and his other works completed during the stay. Meanwhile, I also found time to make eyes at the attractive plump daughter of the house. Now, a quarter of a century later, I could not remember where we had stayed.

By the following afternoon the Dales Way had taken us into Langstrothdale where the surroundings became wilder and emptier and the stream alternately rushed and then rested in pools, its white bedrock contrasting with both deep blue reflections of the sky and clusters of bright yellow flowers along the waterside.

Leaving two of our companions behind in sleepy Buckden, we continued up the valley to our next overnight stop. There had not been a suitable eating place in Buckden, but a pub, not far from the hamlet where we were to stay the night, had been recommended. After the countryside quiet, the sudden noise emanating from the back of this building was most disquieting. Then on arrival we found its yard full of young people in various stages of intoxication, from individuals running around, wrestling and grunting to those sprawled on the ground in drunken sleep. Negotiating our way around the recumbent bodies and dodging the fast moving ones, we entered the bar. The interior was dark, smoky, beer soaked and full of youngsters. After our eyes became accustomed to the gloom, we picked out a harassed lass who appeared to be serving. On asking about a meal, she dismissively waved a hand at her surroundings and irritatedly indicated that she was far too busy to get anything for us. Gladly escaping from this chaos, we then noticed many tents in the meadow behind the building, but never discovered what had been happening here.

In addition to myself, our trio consisted of my youngest son and Tony, a wild looking but actual gentle soul who loved the natural world and old railways, the last for which he was always wanting us to make detours. We now had a problem. Too tired to walk back down to Buckden and return up again, our only option was to eat what we were carrying in our rucksacks. So at a suitable peaceful spot further up the valley warmed by the setting sun, we divided everything we had into three portions. The repast consisted of muesli moistened by lemonade crystals in water, Ryvita slices and ginger biscuits. During this time Matt, always a famous eater, sat down in silence with downcast eyes and arms folded over an empty stomach, in a display of the young's misery at being suddenly deprived of a substantial meal.

On arriving at our overnight lodgings in a remote hamlet higher up the valley, the landlady, on hearing of our predicament, kindly provided us with a pot of tea and a big plate piled high with scones. Then we went outside to enjoy the final sunlight of the day as it highlighted lone outcrops on the opposite hillside.

We were now in high country. Next morning the climb steepened and the surroundings became increasingly desolate, with the few remaining trees clustered together in pathetic little groups. Above Cam Houses we reached the summit of the Dales Way and an old Roman road which now served as the Pennine Way. The view from here was supposed to be wonderful, but due to a hazy atmosphere there was no sign of the proud aloof peaks of Ingleborough, Pen-Y-Ghent and Whernside.

After following the Pennine Way and the watershed of the Pennines for a mile, our route headed down into Dent Dale. Beside the first metalled lane, we rested on a sunny bank. A car was parked on the verge about fifty yards away and its occupant, a man armed with a spade, was digging furiously out on the peat. At the same time he made shifty scrutinising looks in our direction. With the recent Moors Murders fresh in everyone's minds our curiosity was aroused. Then he stopped digging, took a final long look in our direction, dashed over to his car, returned with a large plastic bag and proceeded to shovel the loose peat into it with manic intensity. Carrying the heavily laden bag he even managed a struggling run to his car, before dropping it in the boot and driving away rapidly as though all the police in the North were on his tail. After he had gone, we hoped that the one bag of peat had not cost him a heart attack.

The nearby Dent Head Viaduct of the Settle-Carlisle Railway was imposing. But out of sight to the south, beyond the two miles long Blea Tunnel, this line also passed over the even more impressive Ribblehead Viaduct, its massive size dwarfed by the spacious wild hills on all sides. This hugely expensive project was the result of intense rivalry between railway companies and perhaps should never have been built, but today stands as a monument to the great engineering achievements of those times.

Dent came as a surprise, a cluster of old buildings with roofs set at all angles above cobbled streets. The village's once prosperous hand knitting industry ended with the Industrial Revolution and now it provided us with a large pot of tea and buttered scones in a sunny cottage garden. From here we wandered down to the peaceful River Dee where, apart from insects darting above the gently moving water, stillness and quiet reigned.

The scene changed at Sedbergh and the Howgill Fells. The steep-sided stone walled moors of previous days had been replaced by massive open hills, marking a significant milestone on our journey to the rugged Cumbrian Mountains. During the final two sunny days of the walk, the shining blue hills along the skyline ahead gradually grew in size until each well remembered mountain peak took on its own individual shape. Beyond Staveley this scene was lost for a while behind trees and small rugged hills until a cleft, marking Lake Windermere, opened up to reveal now nearby mountains. Soon we were on the lake shore at Bowness, creating some interest among the crowds of holidaymakers.

When the weather had been hot and sticky on previous days, we had fantasised about the end of the walk as being a time when we would throw off our rucksacks, discard our boots and socks and then run down a clean shelving beach into the Lake for a delicious paddle. Alas,

126

this was not to be. Hereabouts the lake shore was obstructed by jetties and the sunny water displayed the rainbow effects of spilt oil. As the blisters on my feet were now severe, it seemed inadvisable to soak them in this questionable water. So while all of us sat on a jetty eating ice creams, my companions refreshed their steaming feet in cool water while mine could only dangle above.

A special treat came after dinner that evening. Orrest Head, a previously unknown hill, had been pointed out to us. Clearly once favoured by Victorian ladies in their long skirts, its carefully contoured broad paths led gently upwards through trees to a modest summit with a great reward. The blue sky of evening was turning to gold in the west where a bank of shapely clouds hung above the prominent Langdale Pikes. Immediately below us, water of the same pure gold gradually turned to silver further down the lake. It was one of those moments which one wants to last forever. But soon the light drained away and the path down through the dark trees became difficult to negotiate.

Our last expedition before my transfer back to London was around the Peakland Way which John Merrill had pioneered some years before. This proved a fitting end to a decade of walking in this unique region because it reflected all the pleasure which it had given me over this time and long before. The circular Way included everything, from the soft rolling farmland in the south to the bleak moors and gritstone edges of the north and even some less desirable features. The party included my eldest son and his current girlfriend together with two of my walking friends. We started and finished at Hathersage, the nearest point to our North Lincolnshire home. Although the Peak is near many towns and cities and is the first upland on the way up from the South, we encountered few people along the way.

The underlying rocks of all regions determine their

physical appearance. Here, the porous white limestone has been shaped into winding dales while the dour impervious gritstone forms the lovely bleak moors of the northern Peak and notable edges further south. The gritstone areas only support scattered communities, but the limestone parts are notable for their farming, limestone quarrying and frequent signs of a former mining industry. I have long believed that visitors to this country, wishing to take both a long walk and discover the essence of England, could do no better than to take a ramble around the Peakland Way.

Heading southwards from Hathersage, we encountered moorland gritstone edges and passed by Carl Wark, a natural strong point heavily fortified by additional boulders during the Iron Age. The surrounding scene became less severe by the time we reached Chatsworth Park. Here former Dukes of Devonshire had spared no expense in creating a stylised countryside idyll. Beyond the ancient stone circle on Stanton Moor, the gritstone eventually gave way to limestone and our route took us down to Ashbourne, a busy lowland market town and the southern turning point of the Way. Heading back northwards we wandered through the sinuous Manifold Valley flanked by its ever changing limestone outcrops. This was followed by a shockingly sterile region, all that remained of the countryside after extensive limestone quarrying. From there we gladly escaped into Wyedale, a craggy limestone valley, and then followed a string of other lovely Dales leading up to the abrupt end of the limestone country near the Winnats Pass.

The Dark Peak lay ahead, starting with the sliding shales of impressive Mam Tor and beyond to the north loomed the long skyline of Kinder Scout which was approached up Jacob's Ladder. North of this plateau, the Snake Path, a famous but inconspicuous route across a wild, rough and often wet moorland, headed eastwards.

Finally, after passing truncated Hope Cross and climbing up to the airy rocky top of Win Hill, the walk finally returned to the starting point.

One walking era had come to an end and another, very different, was about to begin.

CHAPTER FIFTEEN

SUBURBIA AND FURTHER AFIELD

On my reluctant but not totally unexpected transfer back to London, we chose to live in the pleasant suburb of Northwood. As stated earlier, my childhood dreams of living in the Weald had been swept away by the realities of living in Horley in the early 1960s and neither my wife nor I wished to return to that part of suburbia again. Northwood had a reasonable Metropolitan line service to Central London and in the opposite direction was not far from the Chiltern chalk country. We remained in our new home for the next fourteen years, until then the longest period we had stayed anywhere during our married life and also the longest I had ever lived in one place. By the time we moved to Northwood all our children had left home.

It was important to come to terms with our new situation for, although it had many disadvantages, there were compensations.

London had expanded many times over the centuries but none were as dramatic as the one which began towards the end of the Victorian period. This had been brought about by the introduction of railways, both conventional and underground, which transported workers from their suburban homes to either the City or the West End. These lines spread out from the centre like the spokes of a wheel, and the further out they reached the greater the distance between them. As the housing developments followed the railways, there came a point in-between the ever widening 'spokes' where pockets of countryside were left behind as isolated green areas, and Northwood stood beside one of these.

Rural Middlesex, as I liked to think of our area, lay on ground gradually rising from the Thames towards the Chilterns. Chalk, the underlying rock, was only exposed in one or two local places and elsewhere there was a complex mix of the clays, sands and gravels of the Thames Valley. These variations were particularly evident on path surfaces during wet weather when the going could alternate rapidly between soft mud and firm sand or gravel.

This countryside had never been good farmland and the original rural population was relatively low. However, in one period just before the Metropolis finally descended, there had been limited farming success. That was when it became profitable to grow the fuel for the city's current road transport system, or in other words hay to feed the huge number of horses which hauled the omnibuses, cabs and carts around its streets.

Following the arrival of houses and people, the remaining undeveloped land also underwent some change. The areas nearest to Northwood became golf courses, but even here reminders of the past included decayed barns, a shuttered old farmhouse and the overgrown thorn of former field hedges. The open spaces of the golf courses, dotted with trees and occasional coppices, created attractive scenes, and I liked them best when snow covered the ground, for this not only enhanced their appearance but also meant that golfers and their flying missiles were absent. In the areas close to housing, access for walkers was usually limited to a few public rights of way. With stubborn perversity these often headed at oblique angles across greens and while in transit it was essential to keep a sharp lookout for hard projectiles flying through the air from unexpected quarters.

The true heart of Rural Middlesex was its extensive woodland and most of this lay beyond the golf courses. None of the trees appeared to be ancient and had probably grown on former meadows after farming had ceased up to a century before. The woods nearest to my home gave me immense pleasure over the years, for here it was possible to wander at will whenever there was time to spare and, apart from a dull roar in the background, they provided a complete escape from the clutches of the hateful city. Footpaths ran in all directions through trees, not in regimented rows but in random scatterings of oaks, birches, beeches and other native species. Thick tree cover sometimes gave way to glades, so the ground surface varied from carpets of old leaves, through patches of grasses to jungles of bracken.

At first I wanted to believe that these woods had been part of the ancient forest of Middlesex, a hunting ground of kings. They may well have been so in the Middle Ages, but there was contradictory evidence in the form of earthworks in their midst. These resembled field boundary banks and ditches and were a sign that this had been farm land in the interim. Some old maps of the region eventually came to hand and these confirmed my earlier impression, showing smaller areas of woodland than the present ones. However, one woodland had disappeared in the interim. Known as the North Wood, it was on the site of the modern suburb of Northwood.

As the seasons rolled by, the woods' cycles of pleasure were repeated, from intimate worlds of summer with their contrasting cool leaf shade and sunny glades where crowds of insects danced in the air, to those of winter where distant ever green meadows could be seen beyond the bare trees. At the latter times, the dusty dried-up gullies of summer became wandering winter bournes full of water. The seasons between winter and summer brought birdsong and the bright shiny new greens of spring, and between summer and winter golden dappled leaves fell gently to make a cushioned carpet for walkers. But only the wind and rain, preferably both together, could effectively drown the distant roar of the city and, when this occurred, the nearby hectic metropolis could seem very far away. It always surprised me that although thousands of Londoners lived nearby, these woods were rarely crowded and then only on fine weather summer Bank Holidays. By contrast, on bad weather winter days I often had them all to myself and those were the occasions I cherished most.

While wandering through the woodland's dense summer cover, it was easy to imagine that they extended into the far distance, as they had in ancient days before man came in numbers to settle on this land. But, alas, in reality they were palpably finite. Beyond Bayhurst Wood, the furthest point on my regular short walks, the trees gave way to a prairie without trees or hedges, untypical of the South East's cosy countryside. This pleasing guise hid its former use as sand pits and then as rubbish dumps. One of the very few remaining farms, although on poor land, supported a fine herd of Friesian cattle and some sheep. Elsewhere, farming was still in decline, particularly evident in the neglected fields reverting to scrub land, and if allowed to remain undisturbed these would very soon become native woodland once again. Further away across the Colne Valley and the constricting girdle of the M25, where traffic roared all day and night, arable farming still retained a hold on the chalk hills of the Chilterns.

The River Colne and its valley, the farthest extent of my half-day rambles, formed a natural boundary to my part of Rural Middlesex. Here, the River Colne, a tributary of the Thames, wandered southwards through a flat flood plain from which sand and gravel had been extracted in the past and which still continued to a limited extent. The abandoned workings had become an extensive string of pools known locally as the Lake District. A more appropriate name might have been the Broads, for not only were they of similar origin, but also resembled the Norfolk Broads. Like their East Anglian counterparts they had now become a home for ducks, geese, swans, coots, fishermen and dinghy sailors.

The Colne Valley also provided the route for the Grand Union Canal, once the main traffic artery for bulky goods between London and the Midlands. There were also occasional signs of the old manufacturing industry which the canal had once attracted, the most obvious being metal foundries whose surviving buildings now had miscellaneous uses. In modern times the canal was dedicated to boating, angling and walking. My interest was confined to the last and then only in moderation because lengthy towpath walking can become boring.

Although my part of Rural Middlesex could never be mistaken for genuine English countryside, the rolling chalk uplands of the Chilterns were in view and beyond them at ever increasing distances lay the Midland Plain and the moors and mountains of the North. Alas, the last were far away and not often accessible, but Rural Middlesex was always there on my doorstep to provide an immediate escape from the crowds, bustle and pervasive pollution of Central London.

The Metropolitan Line took me home most days after work. It ran underground before emerging into daylight at Finchley Road and then mounted an embankment. From here massed buildings stretched from one distant horizon to the other. As a country lover, I had to avert my eyes from these sterile scenes because they engendered a crushing feeling of imprisonment. Exactly fourteen miles from Baker Street Station relief came at last with a glimpse of a long rolling wooded skyline to the left of the train. My lovely woods were once again in sight.

Whenever time permitted my wife and I escaped to the nearby Chilterns. These began seven miles to the north and although composed of the same chalk as the South Downs and the Lincolnshire Wolds, their scenery was unmistakably different from both. Here were neither the curvaceous green downland slopes nor the wide empty arable fields of the Wolds, but a mix of trees, woods, pastures and arable fields spread over winding valleys and wide ridges which ultimately climbed northwards to the wooded hill crest.

The Chiltern's proximity to London had become their drawback due to the latter's voracious appetite for growth. After the Second World War, land remaining undeveloped in intermediate areas, including Northwood, was given a measure of protection by Green Belt legislation. However, housing development then leapfrogged over into the countryside beyond, which in the present case was the Chilterns. So although these hills still bore a superficial resemblance to the true rural countryside of sixty or seventy years before, they were now busy with commuters, especially in cars rushing around narrow lanes that had once only known plodding horses and carts. Away from these roads we discovered many peaceful pockets of both arable and wooded countryside. There is another side to every coin and in this case the increased population had led to more footpath usage, with the result that many of these were well sign-posted and maintained.

My wife and I spent many happy hours, both together and with a London-based rambling club, walking through these hills but, rather churlishly, while so doing I often found myself thinking of the parts of England which I loved better and wishing that I could be there instead.

During the early part of the long London period my wife and I returned to the Peak District for a winter walking weekend with our Lincolnshire friends. On arrival the deep snow was thawing and rain carried on the wind from an ominous sky did not augur well. But the white tops of the hills, marching away into grey hazy distance, broken only where dark outcrops and old stone walls pierced through the snow covering, revived all my old longings. There and then I resolved never again to stay away too long from the wild hills which I loved the best. Back in the valley bottom I was drawn like a magnet to an outdoor shop and lying in wait beside the door was a guide to the Cumbria Way. I immediately resolved that this would be my next long distance walk.

A few months later, on a bright cold early May day, my eldest son and I were setting out northwards from Ulverston. The nearby hills already had a miniature ruggedness but we were still half a day's march from the mountains. The Coniston group, dominated by the Old Man, stood out from the long rugged skyline ahead and behind these lurked the grey forbidding Scafell range, on this day wearing snow filled gullies along its sides. The first snow flurries came our way and also draped all the high peaks in white gossamer. We passed Beacon Tarn which, although only at a modest height, had all the characteristics of a high mountain lake. Here, a bitter wind beat ice cold waves onto the nearby rocky shore, and on the opposite side, banks of lifeless brown bracken rose up towards the snow shrouded outline of the Old Man. This scene marked our return to the much-loved Lake District. Later that day, the sun returned to give Coniston Water an icy blue reflection framed by nearby bare tree branches. Yet on the sunnier opposite shore the new season was already under way in the form of multitudinous tree buds creating a fluffy green sheen at a distance.

After a night at Coniston, the walk began through relatively easy going country below the high fells. At midday, the route turned towards Langdale and, while the sun still shone, at Elterwater we fed chaffinches with crumbs from our food. Then a heavy snow squall shrouded the surrounding mountains and valleys alike with white. This covering gave the great Ice Age rock amphitheatre at the head of Langdale, where vegetation has yet to return, an even more forbidding appearance than usual. In the interim I had all but forgotten the sheer majesty of this place. However, our way was not up its mountainous head but to the right over Stake Pass which, beyond a tussocky tundra, took us down to lovely harsh Langstrath. This remote lonely place, one of my most loved high mountain valleys, was surrounded by magnificent desolation apart from a few gnarled old trees beside the beck. From there we passed on to Borrowdale where we spent the next two nights.

The Cumbria Way, apart from its passage over Stake Pass, was essentially a low level route so we decided to give our holiday added zest by spending a day on Great Gable. Although not the highest peak in the Lake District, its striking appearance and dominating position at the focal point of many mountain ranges makes it the queen of them all. We reached the top via Honister Pass, Grey Knotts, where we crossed the snow line, Brandreth and Green Gable. On that day we only came across two other walkers and one of these was a lone old man hobbling slowly along with the aid of a stick over the flank of Brandreth. Afterwards I wondered whether his goal, like ours, had been Great Gable and if he had achieved it.

Great Gable remained hidden for most of the climb and then after breasting Brandreth it came into view as a great forbidding snow-covered dome of crags set against a wild sky. After the final scramble to the summit, the sun emerged and the wind dropped so in relative comfort we were able to enjoy the wide deep scene, ranging from the green depths of Wasdale up to the snowy white heights of Scafell Pike.

As the sun went back behind clouds, the bitter cold wind returned and it was time to go. We moved off down the scree to Styhead Tarn, passing back over the snow line along the way. This tarn, with few signs of vegetation, is always bleak and stark but never more so than on that day. Heading into Borrowdale, I took an admiring look back at the Scafell range against a stormy cold sky before it finally passed from view behind our immediate skyline.

On the following morning a gentle walk took us down the valley to Derwentwater and on to Keswick. The narrow neck of the valley with its bustling river led to a succession of rocky beaches and tree covered headlands bordering the broad water. This lake is my favourite, not only for its intrinsic beauty but also for the beautiful surrounding mountains which, uncharacteristically for the Lake District, stand well back from its edges. For a time these distant snow covered summits seemed to have little relevance as we walked in sunshine surrounded by daffodils, fresh green grass and bursting buds. Then the sky became dark grey and we hastened over the final meadows to Keswick in a storm of hail and sleet.

Leaving the bustle of Keswick behind next day, we climbed behind Latrigg to reach the pass above the Glendereterra Beck. Before the nearby massive slopes finally blocked our rearward view, we looked back at the snow covered mountains through which we had passed on preceding days. At the centre was Great Gable, standing out regal, alone and aloof.

The former masses of rugged rocks through which we had travelled had now been exchanged for smooth steep slopes. However, the one thing that remained was the north wind which met us with venom as we made our way through the narrow valley between the Skiddaw and

Blencathra ranges.

At the top stood the open spaces of the seemingly inappropriately named Skiddaw Forest, where the only trees in sight were a single scrawny coppice next to the weather-beaten lodge known as Skiddaw House. The word 'Forest' once signified 'hunting ground' and not necessarily an area of countryside covered by trees. The heather and bracken of this wide bowl in the rolling hills was briefly spoilt by the messy, noisy, disruption of Carrock wolfram mine. Then an open moor of grass, peat and shining lumps of quartz led us on to the broad top of High Pike, the final northern mountain of the Lake District. It resembled no other in the region, for here we seemed to be suspended in space high above the farmland of the Eden Valley and the coastal plain. Away to the north the hazy hills of Scotland lay on the other side of the Solway Firth and to the east the ramparts of the Pennines stood out in a long snow covered line. The wind, buffeting us cruelly at this exposed place, also propelled marauding snow showers and these continually blotted out sectors of the wide surrounding scene. A gentle slope led from this inhospitable place down past some old mines to a cluster of ancient farm buildings where we spent the night. The remainder of the journey on the following morning was an uneventful lowland walk across farming country to Carlisle.

While waiting for the train on Carlisle Station I made a solemn promise, which regrettably I have not always kept, that I would never let too long an interval of time elapse before returning to the Lakes.

For the first time in our lives we now had the opportunity of taking walking holidays abroad. Some were group holidays, such as those to Bulgaria, Corsica, Greece and Madiera. Others were arranged by ourselves in conjunction with some of my business trips and these took us to more offbeat places, including the Aland Islands in the Gulf of Bothnia, maritime Portugal, the coast and hills around Amalfi in Italy, the Alpen district of Austria, the Greek islands of Aegina and Milos, Schleswig Holstein, the Siebengeberge region of Germany and two separate holidays in the Sogndal and Voss areas of Norway. Again on business trips, but not when my wife was present, I spent a day walking on the Appalachian trail in New England and on another my Norwegian colleagues walked with me to the summit of Gaustatoppen in Telemark.

These excursions each have their own special memories and include those of the huge empty mountain plateaus of Norway and the time in Greece when, faced by the execrable Greek maps, we stopped trying to find our way through that country's version of thorny maquis and let wandering paths take us wherever they chose to go, and once it was to a totally unexpected large ancient temple.

Without doubt the holiday at that period which made the greatest impact was the one to Bulgaria. On a miserable midwinter day we picked it out from a holiday brochure in a moment of rashness. Then having taken the plunge, we then began to hear about its miserable unfriendly people and the poor hotels and our enthusiasm faded away.

Sofia proved to be a bustling city of dull humid heat, where many broken-down cars stood alongside busy roads and also beside the way while en route to the mountains. Both towns and people seemed down at heel to our by now travel weary eyes. As the light faded we arrived at the hills where deciduous trees gave way to pines and heat to welcome cool.

Pamporovo in the Rhodope Mountains turned out to be a purpose built resort of large modern holiday hotels and workers' holiday centres surrounded by big rolling hills with their sides scarred by raw ski runs. With our local government guides we climbed Snezhanka, the nearest big hill, to view many similar forest clad hills rolling away into the far distance. This scene was attractive but not, perhaps, the one that I had hoped for. Some of the view, but we were never sure which, included northern Greece. This part of our tourist map was particularly vague, no doubt deliberately so, because the frontier between the two countries was then part of the Iron Curtain.

Music quickly established itself as a constant background to our holiday. Each morning plangent Eastern-sounding music came into our bedroom from what I understood to be a soldiers' holiday home across the valley. There was bagpipe playing, omnipresent bouzouki tapes in tavernas and restaurants, but most of all we were struck by the unusual plaintive women's singing on folk evenings. By contrast there were also the Beatles songs which belatedly appeared to have just taken the country by storm. So for us, the foreign atmosphere of this country with its traditional peasant agriculture, Orthodox chapels, churches and Muslim mosques all became inextricably intertwined with the Liverpool sound.

Subsequent days were spent wandering through unspoilt forests and the cultivation patches of old mountain villages. It was June and wild flowers were at their best, everywhere providing riots of colour in the bright sunshine. Sadly, every step across these fragile colourful carpets unavoidably crushed their beauty. The scattered villages were mostly constructed of timber framed buildings roofed with tiles or stones. Haymaking was underway, carried out entirely by hand using scythes, rustic forks and rakes and not a single blade of grass was wasted, in marked contrast to the haphazard untidy farming we had seen at the big collectives out on the plains. The workers in the hill villages were mostly middle-aged or older women in peasant dress. Children peeped shyly at us around corners and once an embolded lad mistakenly wished us 'guten tag'. Then at another village a small boy was dispatched from a haymaking group to protect the precious family cow which was grazing close to our path. At that time traditional hand spinning of coarse grey wool seemed to have a comfortable relationship with car maintenance, but I would imagine that since then the new has advanced much further at the expense of the old.

Old military trenchworks of the World War One type first caught my attention near an Orthodox chapel on a knoll, and later I saw more, particularly along what may have been the old Bulgarian/Turkish frontier through the Rhodope Mountains. In spite of their obvious age, it was clear that most of them faced eastwards and may have seen fighting in more than one war. In the nineteenth and twentieth centuries, this nowadays tranquil part of the world was part of the long running sore known as the Balkan Problem.

During that first week the most outstanding event was totally unexpected. It started with an inauspicious bus outing in the company of a party of East German tourists to a village known as Gela. There, marshalled by no less than four official guides, we walked a short distance up to the top of a local hill which presented an excellent view of the Perelik range dominated by the nearby tree covered dome of Karlik. At this point our guides, ski instructors during winter months who never showed much enthusiasm for walking, announced that time was short and the weather too hot to go any further. Then they all sat down for a rest. When two Germans decided to march off and climb Karlik, after momentary hesitation, but perhaps spurred on by international competition, one member of our party and I followed them.

The early stage through cultivation strips was relatively easy. Then the real climb began, hot tiring work up a steep pathless mountainside covered in trees. Perspiration poured off us and we were panting by the time glimpses of sky began to appear through the trees ahead, a sure sign that we were nearing the top. Unfortunately one German, a young man who I later discovered came from Leipzig, had got there before us. In friendly fashion he presented us with scoops of snow from a nearby drift to cool our faces and then we shared the water we had brought along. In front, distant villages and cultivated land shimmered in the heat haze and, behind bare ridges and plateaus with deep snow lingering in sheltered nooks extended into the far distance. In all that seemingly sleeping scene, the only movement came from nearby dancing flies. I have to say that the guides were still enjoying their rest when we finally got back to the bottom.

Having fallen asleep on the bus transfering us to the Rila Mountains, I woke to see distant Musala, the queen of the Balkans, standing regal and aloof in a patchwork quilt of snow above forested buttresses. Borovets proved to be an attractive little place with villas dating back to pre-Communist times as well as some modern hotels and trades union holiday centres. Musala was now our prime target but we did not have to climb the whole of the way as a new gondola lift took us up as far as the Jastrabec Hut. The first stage of the walk was up a gentle slope, passing from scrub pines to high meadows decorated with shy mountain flowers and then to rugged igneous rocks with pronounced glaciation scratches on their surfaces. The last reminded me of my own Lakeland hills as did the summit which stood above several small lakes trapped in ice-carved combes.

As the climb began in earnest, green lichen-clad boulders became interspersed with snow drifts. The final zigzag climb up the approach ridge to the summit and

Musala Hut proved a bit tricky, but when eyes could turn away from the next foothole, there were excellent views across to a rugged saddle and to the final mountain lake now far below.

The summit was marked by a pillar and two motley buildings inhabited by individuals said to be weather men. Their leader provided our party with cups of hot sweet herbal tea in a very basic windowless rest room, somewhat incongruously warmed by a bare single electric bar suspended from above. This gentleman, like his other colleagues on the top of the mountain, was not only very scruffy and untidy, but also appeared to be wearing a pair of bedroom slippers, making a discordant sight among the small crowd of neatly dressed and well equipped hill walkers standing on this small rocky world. The other visitors were mostly Bulgarians, Poles and East Germans. In spite of our very different backgrounds, political systems and language problems, we all came together as friendly like-minded people united in a universal love of the hills.

Shortly after reaching the top, clouds came along and enveloped us in mist, leaving only tantalising half glimpses of distant views. But the satisfaction that we had reached a height of 2925 metres on the highest mountain in the Balkans was enough.

On subsequent days, while wandering through scrub conifers and high meadows, we came across occasional shepherds and cow herders. In this part of the world wandering grazing animals were still cared for by man in the ancient way, a practise once common throughout Europe, but probably survived here only because the Communist East had not advanced as quickly as the West. The clank of cattle and sheep bells both near and far and the sight of roughly clad shepherds, haversacks on backs and leaning on long crooks, provide a poignant memory of that holiday. Once we overtook two shepherds following their sheep and three sadly overloaded pack horses moving slowly up a steep mountain. They were obviously heading for a stint on summer pastures because their equipment not only included grubby bundles but also a portable wood stove complete with its chimney.

Although these foreign trips were very enjoyable, I was always conscious of being a visitor and could never identify with their hills in the same way that I had with those of my native country. In these circumstances it is not surprising that there were often features of foreign hills which reminded me of those at home. The most striking example came on an occasion when I arrived in Athens on a rare cool and very wet day. The hills of Attica, usually exposed and arid, were now for the most part blanketed in cloud and this scene strongly suggested a familiar view of my much loved Kinder Scout.

CHAPTER SIXTEEN

SOUTHERN ENGLISH WALKS

I soon took advantage of our new base for the first of several long distance walks in the South. Although some of these scenes were already familiar to me, most were not.

With my eldest son, I first tackled the Ridgeway, which was the nearest long distance path to my new home. Although its terrain was less challenging than that of many earlier walks, the route fascinated me because it crossed the heartland of ancient England. The walk got off to a most impressive start, but the later stages proved far less interesting.

The winter had not been a bad one and snowdrops, closely followed by crocuses, had come early. Then advance to spring slowed, halted and finally retreated in the face of bitter winds from Eastern Europe. So, after the early flowers had bloomed and faded, they were not replaced by the next seasonal colours. As we set out on our walk at Easter time, both town and countryside alike were grey with cold, but at least the weather remained dry and the sun shone occasionally.

We travelled by train to Swindon and from there a friend gave us a lift to Avebury. On arrival the past immediately commanded the present. We wandered around the huge earthwork, stone circles and processional way in nothing less than awe. Foremost in our minds was the enormous manpower and detailed organisation that would have been required to build this feature, with the primitive stone and bone tools of the time. Its presence also reflected the success of a society based on farming the thin soils of the chalk uplands, in that it had been able to create massive resources over and above those needed for everyday life. We also noted, somewhat wryly, that although the village of Avebury might have encroached on the circle, the medieval parish church had been carefully set down beyond its immediate bounds.

Maybe there are none so deaf as those who can hear but do not understand. On that Avebury morning the noise of chattering squawking birds even drowned the sound of traffic on the main road through the site. The creatures' message seemed to have an underlying urgency rather than the joys of spring. There is a school of thought that believes humans are reincarnated as animals. If so, perhaps the birds that morning were frustratingly trying to tell us, in a language that we cannot understand, what it was like to have been here all those centuries ago.

Long distance walkers on a tight schedule cannot afford to dally overlong in any one place and, reluctantly, we left Avebury behind, following a footpath heading south beside the River Kennet.'s clear waters. Perhaps at the behest of a river god, swirling tendrils were continually weaving voluptuously like dancing girls. Running water, an essential commodity of life, is rare in chalk hills and maybe this explained why Avebury became an important trade and religious centre in early times.

Another surprise waited at Silbury Hill and this was in relation to its size. The grass-covered flat-topped conical mound is the largest prehistoric man made structure in Europe. If the ancients had just built it to command the surrounding scene, they would surely not have placed it in this valley bottom. Presumably, the place had some other special significance, but even after centuries of archaeological work there are only conjectures.

From here we were obliged to follow the busy A40 for a short distance. Originally a main Roman highway, it seemed from the road's orientation that they only recognised the already ancient Silbury Hill as a convenient survey point.

We joined the Ridgeway track at Overton Hill, the start of a route that has remained unchanged for thousands of years. Its survival has to some extent depended on irrelevance to modern traffic patterns, for although the old inhabitants were concentrated on these chalk uplands, the local population nowadays is very small. The chalk hills in this immediate vicinity are unique because large boulders are scattered randomly across their slopes. These sarcens, a name derived from 'Saracen' and originally meaning 'foreign', are the remains of a siliceous layer of rocks which once covered the area and, in due course, provided the stones used at Avebury.

Then we headed up the broad enclosed track running unimpeded for mile after mile over slow, rolling, chalk hills under a big sky. Conditions were ideal for fast walking and, with nothing more than songs of skylarks in our ears, the miles soon fell behind. Hereabouts we met our first fellow Ridgeway wayfarers, an elderly Scots couple. Our brief exchange ended with a traditional walkers' farewell, a goodbye until the next meeting sometime and somewhere on another path. But time is short, paths are many and we rarely, if ever, do.

Towards the end of that day's lonely miles, a distant movement became apparent near Iron Age Liddington Camp. On approach, this proved to be a large tractor with a long-armed trailer spraying a crop of young wheat. The machine stopped near us, the cab door opened and both a young man and loud distorted pop music emerged. We gave him a friendly wave, but he did not respond. Here was the new countryman incarcerated in an iron and glass box totally isolated from the countryside of his forebears.

During that day we went through one large Iron Age fort and passed beside another. More were to be encountered along the way. Following the earlier thought pattern, we again speculated on the tremendous amount of human effort necessary to build them and came to the conclusion that life must have been especially precarious at that particular period of our history.

Next day, as our fence-enclosed route passed across great sweeps of arable countryside, we encountered the first of several muddy messes. In the old days travellers would mostly have been on foot. Now walkers have to share it with a variety of vehicles and large modern farming equipment. From what we could see, the deep ruts on the track matched those turning into and away from adjacent farmland.

Wayland's Smithy, the first of two nearby archaeological sites, was a chambered long tomb constructed around five thousand years ago and already ancient when it acquired its present Germanic name. According to Anglo-Saxon legends, Wayland was a magical smith who made miraculous swords. One mile further on we came up to Uffington Castle, another large hill fort. On the slope below there was the wonderfully simplistic representation of The White Horse, believed to be around two thousand years old, and the nearby prominent conical hill with a flat top was the reputed spot where Saint George killed the dragon.

I have long been struck by the fact that two leaders, with the confusingly similar names of Arthur and Alfred, were involved in comparable military activities in this same neighbourhood. The first, a shadowy Romanised Briton, led a spirited defence against the advancing Anglo-Saxons and the second, around five hundred years later, in a much better recorded clash, halted the invading Danes. Added to this, the massive Iron Age forts along this ridge might also be evidence of other comparable long forgotten clashes between the country's earlier inhabitants and the incoming Celtic peoples. These chalk downs have long been of strategic importance to Britain, a fact that will not have escaped the attention of modern military strategists

So far few people had been encountered along the way, but in the vicinity of Uffington Castle there was almost a crowd. The day was Good Friday and the weather, although still cold, was now sunny. Surprisingly the majority of these were long distance walkers, a circumstance seemingly at odds with their almost total absence elsewhere. Many of those present would have been drawn here by the site's popular curiosity and others because it represented a cogent link with our distant ancestors. In my junior school days, I learnt of the many peoples who had come to this island over the millennia and, as each in turn had taken control, it seemed that their predecessors had disappeared from the scene. Nothing could have been further from the truth and many of today's inhabitants still have the genes of these distant peoples. My personal ancestry, as far as it is known, probably started with the Danes a millennium ago, later to be supplemented by Flemings in the Middle Ages, French Huguenots in the eighteenth century and Scots in the nineteenth. But I very much hope that within me there is at least a small part of the ancient dwellers of England in order to establish my long-term credentials with the countryside I love the most.

As we headed away the crowds disappeared as though by fairy spell. After that nobody was to be seen. Thirst then became an obsession as we marched along with the afternoon's sun on our backs. Nowhere could we find a welcoming cafe or an enticing sign saying 'Teas', and, on the whole, we gained the impression that the locals were not well disposed towards walkers. Two less-than-attractive features of the Thames Valley had now become apparent. The first, consisting of bulky masses rising high into the sky to the north, was Didcot power station and, as we passed through its flume, noxious sulphur dioxide bit into the backs of our throats. The second, the Atomic Energy Research Establishment, was sprawled over former fields at the foot of the ridge.

The next day's walk began much as before along a track across high rolling farmland, but change was soon to come. A first gentle downward slope became a definite descent as the gorse and thicket covered sides of Streatley Common loomed increasingly above. Then there were houses and very busy traffic which spoilt all the natural beauty of this narrow valley where the Thames long ago burst through the chalk ridge. Later, we found peace at South Stoke, first in the form of a sunny, sheltered seat outside a pub, and later, on meadows beside a rippling Thames. Along the way Brunel's brick-built single arch railway bridge received an admiring inspection as did the primitive stark medieval painting on an interior wall of the church at North Stoke.

Although the whole of the long distance path is now known as the Ridgeway, the old name only properly applied to the part west of the river. Eastwards another ancient route, Icknield Street, continued into East Anglia. Although the chalk ridge reappeared on the other side of the river, its scarp was now characterised by gaps, the largest of which provided traffic routes between London and the North. Old travellers, following the line of the chalk hills, always avoided ups and downs wherever possible, so from here onwards old Icknield Street ran across less bumpy ground along the lower slopes of the Chiltern scarp.

151

In this vicinity, the Ridgeway Path was no longer a clear-cut track across the countryside, but a succession of local paths and roads. In addition, we had to divert from it to reach our overnight accommodation. A public footpath shown on our map frustratingly came to an abrupt end at the tall fence of a government establishment, leaving retreat to a busy highway as the only option. Sadly, this was a typical example of the scant regard which official bodies often give to such matters. Walks in an unknown countryside can sometimes lead to very unpleasant places and here a bit of contemporary England included a main road with heavy traffic, research establishments, an airfield and a sewage farm. It is a fact that way-finding through urban scenes is often far more difficult and certainly a lot less pleasing than through uninhabited wildernesses.

Beyond the river the ground rose gradually towards the less interesting Chiltern part of the continuing chalk ridge. The modern Ridgeway Path did not follow the old Icknield Street along the foot of these hills as nowadays this is often a tarmac highway, but passed along a series of interconnecting paths up, down and across the heights above. Stiles, a rarity on the first part of the walk, now became frequent. Other less desirable features were also becoming apparent. As we moved towards outer London, the countryside acquired the characteristics of suburbia in the form of increasingly busy roads and greatly extended old settlements.

Some of the very few walkers encountered hereabouts were close to the chasm where the M40 Motorway charged through the Chiltern scarp and others were near the cement works at Chinnor and its great chalk pits. Next day we passed by Chequers, the house and estate reserved for the personal use of Prime Ministers, which stood in a pleasant vale hemmed in by the broken Chiltern ridge. Then we entered some of Chiltern's beech woods. At the present early season, their sunlit trunks and bare branches reached high above to small buds just about to burst. By contrast at our feet, the dead woodland floor was covered with the remains of last season's dead leaves.

At least one fascinating piece of history came to light along this part of the route. Two millennia have passed since the old British language was regularly used in these parts and in the interim incomers have each brought their own language with them. Consequently, few of today's place names have British origins, but there are occasional surprises and Wendover's was one of them. Its modern spelling proved to be a somewhat disguised form of 'Gwyn Dwr' or 'White Water'. To confirm this description, the clear water of the small stream through the town centre still ran along a bed of white chalk pebbles.

From the Tring Gap, a distant conical hill could be seen against a sombre sky. It was Ivinghoe Beacon and the end of the Way. On approach it became clear that bushes and cold uncomfortable people were standing on the top in almost equal numbers. Projecting above a wide plain, it proved a good ending. In the distance the chalk hills, with a white lion cut into their slope below Whipsnade Zoo, continued on towards East Anglia. On leaving Ivinghoe Beacon in our car, after five days and ninety-three miles on foot, the first rain began to splatter on the windscreen.

The South Downs Way was our next venture. Ever since the end of the 1940s I had never recaptured the earlier joy they had once given me. Now it seemed that if anything was going to do the trick, it would be a walk along their length from Petersfield to the final glorious end at Beachy Head.

The massive Alps and our own gentle southern English landscape may be very different but they are related. The earth movements which created the Alps also caused the previously submerged Wealden rocks, primarily composed of soft chalk and sandstones, to be thrust up into a great dome. In their new elevated position these rocks were rapidly worn away by the elements and only remnants of the original somewhat harder rock crust now stand out as the North and South Downs. The steep scarp slopes of the South Downs face the Weald and behind it gentle dip slopes tail back southwards towards the English Channel. At the western end of these hills there is a substantial coastal plain, but this gradually narrows until the chalk cliffs begin at Brighton. Eastwards from here the sea nibbles ever deeper into the chalk until it finally attacks the main ridge at Beachy Head.

There is always a feeling of unreality at the start of a long distance walk. In spite of all previous planning, it is a time when the task ahead becomes difficult to grasp and boots and rucksack seem heavy, cumbersome and uncomfortable. However, by next day feet and muscles are acclimatised, and at the end of the journey the absence of boots and the daily burden even engender a feeling of near nakedness.

Setting out from Petersfield, the first mix of arable farmland and wooded terrain did not resemble the South Downs as I recalled them, but the well remembered scene returned on reaching the wide open slopes of Beacon Hill. The following night was wet, and next morning, the rain only ceased as we headed back up the now cloud-shrouded ridge and into a small enclosed misty world surrounded by ghostly trees. Here, only delicate wild roses with drops of moisture on their faces provided beauty. A new cool breeze sounded like a distant sea as it stirred adjacent beeches and this, together with the steady plod of our boots and creaks of rucksacks, was all. Compass checks were occasionally necessary to confirm our route and then a wooden sign suddenly emerged out of the murk. In one direction it pointed to Londinium and the other to Regnum. This marked the crossing of Roman Stane Street from London to the South Coast.

However, the ridge track which we were following was the far older of the two ways because it had once been a main road connecting prehistoric farming communities on the Downs. Hereabouts the later Iron Age forts were still evident, but most of the Bronze Age tumuli, meticulously marked on our maps, had recently been ploughed out and were no longer visible, except perhaps from the air. When advances in tool making made farming of the heavier richer soils below the hills practical, the population moved down to present day villages on the Weald. Later, the Downs became sheep walks and so they remained until arable farming returned to the tops during and after the Second World War, but this last was a highly mechanised industry which required few workers. In fact we saw only two farm workers during the whole of that trek and, for that matter, few walkers as well. Like all the other English chalk hills, these regions are now lonelier than they have been since the first farmers arrived here thousands of years ago.

The mist eventually cleared and we looked down to the Arun valley where the river slices through the hills on its way to the English Channel. Absorbed by the wide peaceful scene, we were shocked by a sudden convulsive eruption. A magnificent red deer with fine antlers, who must have been quietly watching us in trepidation, had suddenly reared up from the immediate foreground and went crashing off through a field of ripening barley at high speed. Fascinated, we watched him until out of sight.

Burpham, our destination for the night, turned out to be a pretty little village at the end of a cul-de-sac, complete with a church, shop, castle site and American tourists. Conversation after dinner, conducted by the hotel owners and other visitors, was so snobbish that I grew irritated. Then, taking advantage of a brief lull in the flow, I mischievously suggested that the correct pronunciation of the hamlet's name might not be 'Burffam' as stated but 'Burp-ham'. Reaction was immediate and full of heated denial, but it had the desired effect and afterwards the talk became more temperate.

Next morning after a climb up to Chanctonbury Ring, we sheltered from a cool breeze in the lee of the famous trees to enjoy the sun's luxurious warmth. Peace was total and we eventually dozed. A sudden thunderous noise was accompanied by vibration of the ground. At first my half-awake mind imagined that the large herd of cattle seen earlier was now stampeding. But no, it proved to be no more than two horse riders and their mounts going hell for leather past us and away. Soon come and soon gone, the pervasive peace and quiet of the Downs returned. The dominant solitude of the place, and for that matter along most of the South Downs ridge, was now heightened by very obvious signs of a heavily populated coastal strip only a few miles away to the south. Later, we cruised along through a vast sea of corn where the wind created successions of wandering waves across its surface.

The River Adur passed through the next major gap in the hills. Here, Steyning's old world heart was surrounded by familiar suburbia. Next morning the main road to Shoreham turned out to be busy and unpleasant. By contrast, the dismantled and blocked-up side aisle of nearby St. Botolph's Church showed that the local population had fallen drastically at some stage in the distant past, probably at the time of the Black Death. Next, the distant large chapel of Lancing College caught the eye. Although attractive, its severe lumpy shape seemed quite at odds with the gentle surrounding countryside. Devils Dyke, a long deep combe in the scarp slope of the Downs, was our nearest point to Brighton. One of the few busy spots along the route, its car park was full, the cafe and pub were open and a crowds of sightseers were watching the amusing antics of novice hang gliders.

This was not our scene so we hurried on, soon to be engulfed by thunder and heavy rain. In a trice all was transformed, including the surface of the Way which now became the all but forgotten glutinous chalk mud of the past. Then we had a confrontation. In the current vicinity the track was enclosed by new tall barbed wire fences and, what is more, a group of cows without a herder could be seen approaching from the opposite direction. Horror upon horror we then spotted a large bull with a ring through its nose in their midst. Based on past traumatic experiences and with visions of being crushed against the barbs or something worse, we rapidly removed our rain gear and rucksacks, threw them over the wire and then gingerly eased ourselves through the barbs. The operation was completed just in time before the mass of animals arrived. As we looked on, they passed slowly by without giving us the benefit of even a passing glance.

The rain passed away and we emerged onto thick, short turf leading up to the top of Ditchling Beacon. Views from this high point were wide, but the most impressive sector to the east contained tall Seaford Head, a timely reminder that ahead the sea cliffs were not only getting closer but also gaining height. By late afternoon the sun came out again and we sat for a while in its warmth listening to the omnipresent song of larks.

The next day's twenty miles of walking traversed three groups of downs. We were now in the vicinity of Lewes, the scene of my happy, boyhood holidays. However, the well remembered prominent clump on Black Cap had now gone, replaced by a less tall but greater number of trees, and much of the surrounding grassy hillsides had since become arable land. Sadly, only the deep combes in this vicinity remained in their original lovely wild state. In one of these my old uncle, in true Boy Scout fashion, had once tried to reheat cold tea by pouring it into a cream cracker tin and warming it over a small fire which he had kindled. The result was not successful, but the incident had remained as a quixotic memory of a long gone carefree time.

On the top of Kingston Down we met our very first fellow long distance walker along the route. Ahead lay the flat flood plain of the lower Ouse Valley with its treeless grey green sea marshes and to the north Lewes guarded a strategic gap in the hills. We ate our lunch beside an ebb tide river at Southease and later made our way over the bare flanks of Itford Hill and Firle Beacon to our next overnight stop.

On the last day we first came to the pretty, but nowadays commercialised, village of Alfriston in the Cuckmere Valley. In sharp contrast, the lower reaches of the River Cuckmere could be unique in southern England, for there is no road, no bridge and no nearby buildings. Instead, the river wanders through flat meadows before encountering the seashore at a shingle bank flanked by white cliffs of old England. Perhaps accentuated by the dull day, the brighter light at the seashore at first seemed dazzling. The Way then became a switch back over the eight Seven Sisters. The turf at the bottom of each dip was burnt brown by salt spray, contrasting with higher stretches where blue wild flowers grew in profusion. At nondescript Birling Gap, the teashop owner bemoaned his poor season while we drank several cups of hot sweet tea in quick succession. The final climb of the walk took us to the top of Beachy Head where, in sharp contrast to preceding days, we found ourselves among a crowd. There was also more humanity, far below, where a convoy of laden launches had come out from Eastbourne to conduct an inspection of Beachy Head's cliffs and lighthouse.

The path turned sharply and we descended the steep scarp slope of the Downs for the last time. The sprawl of Eastbourne lay below and beyond, to the east, a low flat coastline curved away to the horizon. The Way finished at the entry to a road where it was marked by a map board. Nearby two people were buying ice creams at a kiosk.

That holiday was notable for its peaceful gentle scenes in an otherwise busy part of the world. However, the magic that I had found here as a young boy had only returned as occasional faint echoes. In truth, a middle-aged man could never again see things through the eyes of a child. The weather remained dull all day but, as we travelled back to London to join its ever restless traffic, crowds and babble of tongues, that did not matter any more.

Throughout the London period and whenever time permitted I walked with groups, my wife and sons and sometimes alone. Anything from short local walks to long treks in distant places all provided wonderful antidotes to life and work in a hectic metropolis and tiring overseas travel.

During this period, I only undertook one other long distance walk in Southern England and that was one which led me around part of the Thames Basin. My Oxfordshire Way walk took place shortly before retirement and also during high summer. In fact the weather was so warm and the ground so parched that I could have been walking across a hot, dry, country far away to the south. Such is the unpredictable nature of walking in England!

Bourton-on-the-Water, the starting point, stood astride the River Windrush, the first Thames tributary encountered. The village stood on the dip slope of the Cotswolds, away from the prominent edge overlooking the

Vale of Severn, and here the surrounding hills were only very gentle. The rock of the region, my old familiar Jurassic limestone, provided the building material for many attractive older dwellings along the route and also for the walls bounding fields. Although the former were often delightful, for me on that walk they were more important for the moments of welcome shade which they provided.

There were few occasions during a lifetime's walking in England when the weather was so consistently hot and dry. The combination of hot air trapped around multitudinous stalks of ripening cereals and the sunlight reflected from their shining seed cases made each field crossing all but unbearable. Now the once persistent muds of winter had become piles of dust which rose in clouds at every step. This might well have been a populated countryside, but it was one which had become extremely quiet and still in the pervasive heat. Hardly a sound was to be heard anywhere, even from settlements which I passed through during the baking middle of the day. In these circumstances, it took only a brief chirrup of a lone bird in a bush or the distant solitary clank of metal against metal to capture my attention. It seemed that the whole land was taking a long siesta while I alone marched on. Shade became a rare commodity, especially when the sun was high and the shadows small. Whenever my eye sought out the way ahead, it took conscious note of any shady spots beneath trees or beside hedges for brief respites. I believe I would have to walk this Way many times over before again encountering similar conditions.

During walking hours my thirst was prodigious. Not only did I carry my usual one litre bottle of water, but also had extra ones strapped to the outside of my rucksack. Even so, supplementary supplies often proved necessary and I kept a constant look out for possible watering holes in the form of pubs and village shops. Unfortunately, in modern times, these were becoming rare in the countryside. I am not a pub person, but it became essential to patronise these institutions during the present trip. Lack of familiarity may have made me more conscious of my surroundings, because I soon observed that the pub patrons were of two broad types, the majority of the first being encountered during the early part of my walk and the second during the latter. The first type of patron wore nondescript everyday clothing and said little apart from uttering a few words in between long silences. These statements, seemingly little more than a short series of unintelligible grunts, must have been of import to the listeners because they usually brought nods of approval. In brief, these pubs were cool, restful, places which provided welcome sanctuaries from the heat outside.

The second type of pub patron was notable for smart 'country' clothing of which one or more items were green. In addition, everyone spoke simultaneously in loud commanding voices, with nobody apparently listening to what was being said. Consequently, the racket was terrible. It did not take me long to conclude that these patrons were thinly disguised suburban commuters choosing to play what they conceived to be a rustic role in their spare time. Whether true or not, I could not stand these places and on one occasion chose to face the heat and thirst outside rather than the pandemonium within.

From Bourton, the way passed through low rolling fields leading down to the Evenlode Valley which I then followed for many miles to reach the large park surrounding Blenheim Palace. As an admirer of country houses which enhance their surroundings, I found this flamboyant pile totally at odds with the gentle surrounding countryside. After a night at Woodstock, the Way then led me on a wide curve through countryside to the north of

Oxford, at a distance which gave no hint of the nearby city. During that day I encountered a feature unusual in this general scene. It was Ot Moor, a large dead-level badly-drained fen set in a shallow basin below higher ground. When young I believed that 'moor', a word first encountered in books, was descriptive of dark wild hills, little realising that it was related to 'morass'. In reality it can describe any boggy place, whether in wild hills or tamed lowlands. As a boy, the only descriptive names I knew for familiar wet lowland places were 'fens', 'marshes' or 'carrs'.

By late afternoon I arrived at Waterperry House with gardens open to the public. There might have been a special function that day because teas were being served in a marquee. However, most of the crowds had gone when I charged in and ordered the largest possible pot of tea and a big jug of cold water to go with it. The young waitress at first seemed flabbergasted, but then rose to the occasion and provided both. I drank the lot. With six miles still to go, the cool of evening proved a boon, but I was very tired on reaching my overnight resting place at Tetsworth. The long soaks in baths after each of these hot energetic days were among the most pleasurable I have ever known.

The limestone country was now behind and the prominent scarp of the Chilterns stood ahead. As the only significant hills along the route, they were a cogent sign that I was now approaching my home area. For several miles the Way crossed fields and passed along lanes parallel to the Chilterns as if trying to avoid the inevitable, and then, taking the bull by the horns, headed straight up to the crest of the ridge at Christmas Common. All that now remained was a walk through woods, along rounded chalk valleys and past occasional small hamlets to arrive at Sunday afternoon busy Henley-on-Thames, where my wife was kindly waiting to drive me back home.

Life is a series of challenges, great and small, exhilarating and disagreeable. Walking is the one which I enjoy most, but there was no prior inkling that the gentle Oxfordshire Way would prove to be such a major one.

CHAPTER SEVENTEEN

SOUTH WESTERN WALKS

Until the 1980's my knowledge of the South West had been limited to the hitch-hiking holiday to Lands End with Norman in 1951 and two seaside holidays with our young children during the early 1960s. Although my memories of Exmoor in 1951 were very pleasant ones, I had never got around to returning. The reason was that in earlier days my ambitions were directed towards regions which were more rugged and accessible than the South West. However, tastes change on growing older and, although my passion for wild lonely places remained strong, I had now acquired an additional interest in the marginal lands of England where the tides of settlement have ebbed and flowed over the centuries.

Over the years, my wife and I had stayed at a number of Holiday Fellowship and Countrywide Holiday Association centres, mostly in the North, and had thoroughly enjoyed the accommodation, walks programmes and social activities which these provided. After our move to London, I reminded my wife of my earlier pleasurable stay in Exmoor, and as a result, we took a short break at the Holiday Fellowship Holnicote Centre in the Vale of Porlock, and this kindled our interest in Exmoor further.

Exmoor's big hills tumbling directly into the sea were just as I had remembered them, but now we also found much more in the form of open moorland, extensive oak woodlands, busy streams and rivers, lovely steep valleys, pretty villages, many sign-posted and well maintained footpaths and, above all else, friendly local people. Although now a National Park, it differed in one important respect from the Peak and Lake District Parks of modern times in that it had remained a quiet part of the world. In addition, this part of Highland Britain had a climate significantly better than that of other similar regions further north.

By the end of that holiday the region had begun to grow on us. Then fate played a hand. Our next door neighbours in Northwood had just bought a cottage in a village between Exmoor and the Quantocks and they kindly invited us to stay in it from time to time. It was an offer that we could not refuse and went there several times over the years.

After this first holiday I thought that a long distance circular walk might be based on Exmoor and, as none existed at the time, I devised a tentative one. So, on a fine but cool spring day in 1981, my youngest son and I set out from Minehead following the Exmoor Coast westwards.

After a steep climb through trees above Minehead harbour, then dry at low tide, we reached open moorland high above a misty blue sea where an invisible ship's fog horn sounded at intervals. A long, gently undulating moorland plateau, which we later identified as typical of Exmoor, ended with a steep drop down a rocky valley where gorse was in full bloom. Then a lane through old world Bossington led out to a path on the landward side of the shingle bank across Porlock Bay. In 1996 this bank was breached during a bad storm. The former freshwater marsh became a salt one where every tide since has flowed in and out and the path was lost. This event provided a graphic reminder of how scenes, especially those along our coasts, are always changing.

The former path led to the little port at Porlock Weir, where that day we ate our sandwich lunch in a sunny sheltered nook on the quay. A place of great contrasts, high wooded hills loomed over a freshwater marsh and spring flowers bloomed in cottage gardens backed by a stark, sea-washed, shingle ridge.

On returning to steep wooded hills falling into the sea, we reached the small hamlet of Culbone. Massed daffodils bloomed beside its diminutive church and here we enjoyed a pot of tea outside one of the two surviving cottages. Then, emerging onto high green pastures above the trees and the sea, we wandered along paths and tracks between scattered farms. Winter was over, lambs and bright green grass were both growing apace, bushes had just broken into new leaf, larks sang and even the sea had a gentle summer murmur.

We left the coast at Yenworthy to cross over the hill into the East Lynn Valley. Bracken and heather gave way to meadows at the bottom and here the warmth of that day's sun still lingered as shadows lengthened. At Oare Church we ruminated on Lorna Doone and John Ridd, just as Norman and I had done some three miles downstream thirty years before. Our overnight stop was nearby and next morning we followed the Lynn downstream into a tree-enclosed defile where the river soon became a turbulent torrent. When Norman and I were here on that autumn day long ago, the weather had been gloomy and misty but now, with the naked branches of the sessile oaks allowing bright sunlight to penetrate through, the ground was a mass of reds, browns and yellows from a combination of the previous seasons growth, the fresh colour of stones shattered in the recent winter frosts and the new season's primroses.

We arrived in Lynmouth, a lovely mountainous place, as it basked in the bright coastal sunlight, with its cherry blossom in bloom and fresh painted buildings waiting for the summer season. Leaving by the cliff railway, we then took to the North Walk, with its weather sculpted pinnacles above, sea battered cliffs and boulders below and the nearby herd of feral goats all vying for our attention. Later, through the masses of budding trees along the coast road, there were occasional glimpses of wooded hills tumbling onto rocks and a blue sea flecked by white horses. From Woody Bay, a well made track bordered by flowering gorse then led down into steep sided Heddon Valley where we had lunch at the Hunters Inn. Here the coastal scene underwent a radical change. Trees disappeared, apart from a few scraggy survivors sheltering in deep gullies, and our route now ran between the edge of rough meadows and a steep slope above the sea. Finally large and high Great Hangman and the lesser but more shapely Little Hangman led us on to our next night's stop at Combe Martin.

At the western end of the National Park, we turned inland. Combe Martin's long drab main street led us on to quiet country lanes and the village of Paracombe. But even so there was still some way to go before open moorland was reached at Chapman Burrows. Here, winter still lingered and a free ranging cold wind brought tears to our eyes. With the heather still shrivelled brown, only the yellow of the previous season's lank grasses provided some colour to contrast with the blue of the sky. Undulations were crowned by Bronze Age tumuli and these, together with the impressive Long Stone, provided our waymarks through the solitude.

The pleasure ended on reaching fenced roads and enclosed moorland converted to inferior grazing. The farm where we stayed that night was one of several carved out from the ancient Exmoor Forest by the wealthy Knight family in the nineteenth century. At this cold austere place the first signs of summer had yet to come, but the family who lived here with their Galloway cattle and sheep could not have been more welcoming.

The new morning's brilliant sunshine lit up a sparse landscape. A track led down to the Barle Valley at Cow Castle, a prehistoric fortification perched on a pronounced natural hillock. This was the best part of that day, a time of sharp light, sparkling cold running water, pine woods and open moorland, which was home for a herd of lovely russet Exmoor ponies. But all the while the scene was slowly changing as the river moved down into softer regions. Below Withypool, the gently rippling water meandered through parkland glades before the valley sides closed in. Then massed trees vied for space and the stream alternately dashed over rocks before resting for a while in still pools. The ancient clapper bridge at Tarr Steps came next. Unique on Exmoor, it is said that the Devil constructed it and he likes to sunbathe here whenever the weather is fine. As the day wore on the weather became increasingly cloudy and cold, muting birdsong and our own spirits. Finally, we left the River Barle to spend the night on the southern edge of Exmoor, overlooking rolling green Devon farmland.

Next day, the sky was dull and the wind bitter as we turned north on the last leg of our journey. From bustling chilly Dulverton, we initially followed a sheltered lane over hills before emerging into a cold searching wind that only moderated on reaching Winsford. We left this village along the upper Exe Valley, a place of narrow meadows flanked by grass, trees, bracken, seasonal golden gorse and occasional rock outcrops, a varied scene which became delightful when the sun finally emerged. We sat for a time in sheltered warmth and peace until it was time to follow tracks and paths to Exford, the final overnight stop of the holiday.

Morning arrived with bright sunlight, no wind and a

white frost. The gentle hills, meadows and trees around the village belied its elevated position so that only a modest climb past meadows and moorland brought us to the top of Dunkery Beacon. On this morning Exmoor's highest point was king with all the world at its feet. From the immediate stark stony moor, the ground fell away southwards to a mosaic of green fields and, to the north, moorland incised by winding, wooded valleys led towards a hazy glimpse of blue sea beyond. We stayed here for some time absorbing the sun, peace and views. The descent then led us through heather, followed by bracken interspersed with golden gorse and finally at the hill bottom, past delicate birches just coming into leaf. All the way down, the only sounds apart from our own footsteps were the omnipresent song of skylarks, a very gentle breeze and, for the first time that spring, the summery buzz of bees. Yet a week later England was in the grip of the worst spring snow blizzards for decades.

Wootton Courtenay was memorable for its deep red soil and a cool drink in the sunny, warm pub yard. We then stopped for lunch part way up the last climb of the holiday, watching a slow motion world of people and animals in the sun below. Then we passed along the open ridge where Norman and I had battled with the vicious wind in 1951. Beyond busy Dunster, tranquillity again returned on rich green marshes where the only visible creatures, gently grazing cattle, were set against the seeming landlocked buildings of Minehead. Finally we climbed over a bank onto a wide sandy beach and followed it into the town.

People are as much an integral part of walks as places and on this journey we met all sorts, from locals to holidaymakers, Cockneys to possible aristocrats, shabby, hard-working hill farmers to individuals clad in very smart 'country' clothes and highly polished brown shoes or boots. Having not encountered the last before, we were puzzled until discovering that they were vehicle-borne hunt followers.

One special memory of that trip is of an ill-lit sparsely furnished tap room in one of the hill villages. The bar, dark and gloomy, occupied much of the room. Although its capacious shelves contained few bottles, barrels equipped with large brass taps and mounted on trestles occupied a great deal of space. In this setting a group of presumed locals were conversing in what seemed unintelligible strings of sound which always began with something like 'aw, agh, aw, agh, agh' and usually finished with 'ho,ho,ho'. We listened, but did not understand a single word, and here we were only one hundred and fifty miles from London!

The walk had been most enjoyable and the scenic beauty often exhilarating. Most importantly it had taught me more about Exmoor. That education was to continue during the months and years ahead until I understood why some parts of our long walk, particularly those along the coast, had been delightful, while others, mainly across some of the inland areas, had proved rather disappointing. In truth inland Exmoor is a shy countryside, only revealing its best to those who have come to know it well.

On first encountering Dartmoor, the marked differences between these two nearby uplands proved striking. The first of these was their rock structures, Dartmoor with its granite and Exmoor with its sandstones, and the second their relationship, or lack of it, with the sea. Thirdly, Dartmoor's best was always on display, usually in the form of hills culminating in rocky tors, while Exmoor's generally have flattish tops. Perhaps this is the main reason why Exmoor, apart from a few well publicised honeypots, remains peaceful while Dartmoor can simultaneously be crowded. Yet Dartmoor has no delightful coast like that of

Exmoor's and also suffers from the intrusive army firing ranges which have been thrust upon it. I have yet to find a satisfactory answer to this puzzle.

After the excursion around Exmoor, I decided to take my first look at Dartmoor. This was a lone walk following an erratic course. On arrival at Exeter's St. Davids Station, I gave the taxi driver a £5 note and asked him to take me as far as possible in my chosen direction. In due course, he dropped me off at a point where the River Teign emerged from a steep-sided, wooded valley.

By late afternoon, the narrow tree-clad trough opened out into undulating pastures. A nearby tractor was turning over rows of new cut hay in the hope that they would dry before the next rains came. Yet even without the sun this scene was an evocation of summer pleasures gone and those yet to come. But modest pleasure could not mask some disappointment because the wild hills which I sought were nowhere in sight. On peering again it was apparent that there were two distant green hills with rocky outcrops on their summits, neither of which was impressive. At the beginning of this, my first trip, I began to wonder whether my preconcieved ideas about Dartmoor, mostly gained from books, might be wrong. While approaching Chagford for the overnight stop, thoughts of the first day's modest pleasures were tinged with doubts about those of the morrow.

Leaving Chagford's quiet market place on a bright sunny morning, intimate lanes took me along the upper reaches of the River Teign. For a time views were limited to nearby lush vegetation and then a fleeting glimpse of green distance proved disturbing. There was no horizon, for where it should have been only thick grey mist prevailed. Finally, the lane climbed from the valley to pass beside a field of near-ripened wheat, something that I had never seen before at this height in England. Beyond a gate

I passed onto to a rising rough meadow populated by cattle, sheep and ponies. At a point on the climb the sense of enclosure, prevailing since starting out that morning, suddenly gave way to one of space. Turning rearwards a patchwork of small fields and trees could now be seen reaching back into the distance. A few further steps took me to the top of the rise and ahead were the hills which I sought.

Emptiness ranged in horizontal layers led on to seeming infinity. The first and lowest of these, a shining light green, led up to one of darker hue and then on to sombre grey under a thick canopy of mist. Far above, dazzling vapour rose to heaped white clouds in a blue sky. Greeness, above all else, was the most striking feature of this scene. Long familiar with drab moors only relieved when heather bloomed, I now found myself on a verdant prairie. Overwhelmed by the view, it took some time to absorb the details. At first, sheep seemed to be scattered throughout the greenery and, later, some of these turned out to be an ancient stone circle. I stood entranced at this wide scene for a long time before moving on.

The sun disappeared on approaching the bank of mist and there I met a small family group beside abandoned intakes. After small talk about the weather, they went southwards into good visibility and the youth hostel at Bellever while I headed up the slope towards Sittaford Tor and into clammy mist. My compass, map and watch were now my only guides as the visibility and light intensity changed constantly, but never became better than poor. Walking on through this featureless scene, my sense of the distance covered went awry. Change when it came was unexpected. The ground in front began to fall away. Then the curtain of mist drew aside and I immediately knew where I was. Below, a rock-strewn East Dart River curved away along the bottom of a steep, wild valley, typical of the places which I had come to love over the years. Away from the clammy chill of the tops, I ate a peaceful lunch in the sole company of dancing river water.

Back on the tops, the mist had lessened with visibility now ranging no further than clumps of grass at my feet to modest featureless distance. Higher White Tor, the next height along my way, suddenly loomed out of the murk. Even from the top of this sturdy granite pile there were no distant views, only grey opacity, apart from a buzzard riding on the wind, a sure sign that there was more wildlife around here than was visible to my eyes.

The mist fell away on approach to the upper West Dart valley. Here, the small battered trees of Wistmans Wood provided a welcome sight after many empty miles. I rested beside the gnarled oaks, watching occasional humanity wandering up to this tourist attraction, much loved by artists for its' combination of massed contorted branches and harsh rocks. Later, I turned off the track into a grassy den surrounded by bracken. Comforted by now knowing my exact position, daydreams changed to dozing and I slept until the cool of late afternoon roused me to move on.

My only excuse for what happened next was remaining half asleep. I walked up to the hotel crowded with tourists sunning themselves outside and eating cream teas within. Possibly through boredom, they seemed to find me an object of great interest. I walked into the hotel, and after wearily removing my boots addressed the receptionist.

'I have booked bed and breakfast for the night.'

She looked blankly at me and checked her records. 'No, you have not.'

I repeated my opening statement and she again denied all knowledge of it. All while the idle bystanders looked on with increasing interest.

Preparatory to delivering a broadside I said 'Surely this is the Such and Such Hotel!'

The answer was immediate, final and totally deflating. 'No it is not. That place is a mile up the road.'

The mistake could hardly have seemed possible, but I had managed it. By now under intense scrutiny from the assembled throng, I replaced and clumsily retied my boots, a seeming endless operation, before making a most undignified retreat. The only thing to add is that my actual hotel proved to be an excellent one.

Next day's leisurely walk took me to Dartmoor's south western edge. The morning was bright and dewy and on Crockern Tor my boots left a clear trail through the grass. By comparison, Princetown and its prison were most disagreeable, and it was only after hastening to the delightful view from the summit of Great Mis Tor that I could put it out of my mind. From this high point, waves of long green moors reached northwards like a petrified ocean and I, drifting randomly across them like a piece of flotsam, finally came to rest in the space between two of these green lines representing the nascent River Walkham. This stream led me down past the remains of a Bronze Age settlement to increasingly lush lower moorland, then to neglected overgrown farmland and finally to my next night's lodgings in Horrabridge.

After overnight rain, the new morning was cloudy and humid. Damp country lanes took me to the edge of the wilder country at Burrator Reservoir. On arrival the sun emerged for the first time and for a brief moment of glory all the rain droplets on the petals of the wild flowers sparkled like diamonds. Then the moors closed in on me along the track to Warren House in the upper reaches of the Plym Valley. Perspiring heavily, I clambered up to the plateau wilderness, resting for a while on Hen Tor where the only sounds were those of a gentle breeze and my own heavy breathing.

Broad, grassy tops interspersed with peat beds now lay ahead. The prominent tors of preceding hours had all but gone, confirming a tentative conclusion that I reached on preceding days. The tors of Dartmoor are justly famous because they are impressive and, more importantly, often accessible. However, from the large central moorland plateaus they often appear as cowering features along valley sides and moorland edges. The heart of Dartmoor, far from popular conception, is a place of great empty space and solitude. After lunch beside a hilltop cairn I made my way down to the hamlet of Hartford and then on to Ivybridge. By then my thirst had grown into the only thing in the world which mattered.

Ivybridge was my southern turning point and next day I planned to walk northwards to Hexworthy in the heart of the moor. There had been no rain overnight, but the weather forecast was poor, so the prospect of a trek across extensive featureless country in bad weather was not appealing. Even so two encouraging signs had become apparent. First, cloud cover appeared to be lifting from the lower hills and, second, my route proved to be along the track of an old mineral railway. Its easy gradients and the firm footing on the former ballast provided fast walking conditions and I soon arrived at an old abandoned mine near the headwaters of the Rivers Erme and Avon. Here, a path through spindly heather led to the summit of a pyramid-shaped tip which presented a view of the ground ahead. Disconcertingly there did not appear to be any path across the intervening marsh to my next way mark, Aune Head, identifiable as a nick on the skyline.

Moving cautiously across the wet ground, I carefully avoided half-hidden potential ankle twisting holes in-between clumps of marsh grass. Then conditions improved while making my way along the drier sections of old medieval tin workings, but these led me into a marsh. A single stride took me from soft but safe footing into total insecurity and with it came the sudden nightmarish thought that on sticking in this soft mass, there would be nobody around to help me get out. As it was, I just managed to twist round and leap back before falling.

The relatively secure edge of the morass then led me away from my chosen route. Realising that it was necessary to cross the Aune Stream in order to reach the other side of the marsh, I tried to reach it three times and failed. On the fourth I finally arrived at the river's edge. It was about five feet wide and the opposite bank appeared reasonably firm. I jumped. The clump on which I landed toppled, taking me with it. Although my legs were immersed in water, I realised with relief that its bed was firm. Clambering out, I then sqelched away northwards towards Aune Head.

During this trying time I had not noticed that the sky was becoming brighter. At one moment the ground ahead was still rising and at the next a wide panorama of sunlit green hills were rolling towards prominent distant tors. There was also an obvious track which would lead me out of the moor.

Most of my prior Dartmoor knowledge came from the nineteenth century writings of William Crossing, a local man with a lifelong passion for the Moor. Hexworthy had been one of his haunts, but the simple hostelry which he had known and where I planned to stay for the night, had been replaced by an impersonal hotel, the only significant change in a scene which otherwise would have been the same since his day and probably for centuries before.

Next morning a well used track took me through the heather along Hameldown Ridge. To the south, impressive tors stood out against the sun and, to the north, green ridges rolled away into the distance. Even Princetown, prominent on its hilly eyrie some eight miles away, appeared pleasing at this distance. The combination of beauty, space, sun, cool breeze and excellent walking conditions generated great pleasure combined with a sense of freedom.

Pleasure is heightened by knowledge that it has to be finite. Time moved on and with it came change. The sun acquired a halo and there was now a mass of angry cloud along the western horizon. Beyond the ancient village of Grimspound, the ground fell away towards the east. Heather gave way to bracken and then to grass, on which a large herd of lowland cattle were feeding. Beyond them a gate marked the end of the hills.

In the new warm scene away from the wind and facing the best of the morning's weather still in the eastern sky, I followed deep country lanes to Moreton Hampstead. At the end of an energetic walk, I sat down for a rest on a low wall at the bus station. From here the hills were no longer visible. Now seeming a world away, I could picture them accepting the advancing rain as they had on countless other occasions over the centuries.

In recent days I had gained much enjoyment from these unique hills and, although there could never again be the eager anticipation of a first timer, they have since always given me the pleasures of sun, wind, mist, rain, peace and wide quiet spaces in full measure.

CHAPTER EIGHTEEN

RETIREMENT

With every day a busy one, the years passed by almost unnoticed and then, suddenly, it was time to think about retirement.

The idea that final years at work would be a gentle slowing down process proved mistaken, for not only was I coping with increasing work and the frustrating delays of commuting into and out of central London, but was also dashing over to Continental cities at frequent intervals. In these circumstances I looked forward to retirement as a welcome relief from my current lifestyle and a time when my wife and I would be able to do more things together. I also knew that it would finally give me the opportunity for a type of long walk not previously possible.

At work there had been satisfaction in filling various positions to the best of my ability and in making a positive contribution to the manufacture of the fuels and chemicals on which our modern society is based. Even during the early days I was aware that many fuels had undesirable environmental effects, but at the time there always seemed to be practical steps to counteract them. However, during the last fifteen years of my working life, the level of carbon dioxide in the earth's atmosphere, which had been rising since the start of the Industrial Revolution, was identified as the main contributor to the earth's greenhouse effect which could lead to both climate change and rising sea levels. The only solution to this problem was to reduce the world's fossil fuel consumption, a task far easier said than done. It proved a sad note on which to end my working career.

The key decision facing my wife and myself at this time was the location of our home in retirement. Although my wife had made a life for herself in Northwood, I had not. For me our home in the suburbs was basically a place to sleep at night and rest at weekends. Neither of us cared for the South East, so the time had come to look elsewhere. This was to be the first time in our married life when we had free choice of where we would live.

My wife had left Nottingham many years before and had no desire to return. Although we had lived happily in Lincolnshire more recently, even there circumstances had changed. Also, my long standing love-hate relationship with my home county left me with no pressing desire to return there except as an occasional visitor. At heart, although my roots were in my home county, I disliked it for being a predominantly man-made region. Other considerations were that we did not want to live too far away from our children and their families and also wanted to be in an area that would attract them at holiday times.

A number of alternatives were considered. The Weald, which I had loved as a boy and where I had once hoped to live as an adult, had undergone great change because London had crept out and enveloped it. We considered Swansea where we had a happy time in the early 1960s, but this once laid-back last big town in the west had now turned into a busy metropolitan one. Derbyshire had been an ideal holiday location both before and after I met my wife, but neither of us regarded it as a place to live.

Then there was Lakeland which had given me much joy since my first visit in 1951. Having picked out Keswick as a possible place to live, I had a most unpleasant thought. We might choose to live there because we could walk on nearby mountains whenever we chose, but a day would surely come when, due to infirmity, we would no longer be able to climb them. The thought of constantly seeing these hills and never being able to reach their tops was something which I knew I could never face.

We had recently become drawn to Exmoor. For here was a region which was both dramatic and gentle, wild and tamed, and beautiful and bleak, and all of this was to be found in a very small compass. Typical examples were pretty old villages with colourful flower gardens and tea shops which were not far from bare, windswept tops with their lank grass and dark, out-of-season heather. Then there were the numerous small valleys leading down to the sea. Inland these were warm lush places where vegetation and wildlife prospered, but seaward, bleak hills towered above stark rocks and cliffs. Most importantly, Exmoor did not have the problem which I had identified with the Lakes. For although an upland region, tarmac roads passed close to many of its high places.

Exmoor had another attraction which assumed greater importance as I grew older. When young I was always drawn to the wildest places and while relishing them, at first I chose to ignore any signs that might have suggested otherwise. In the end this pretence became insupportable because man had been around for so long and in such numbers in Northern Europe that all its physical features, flora and fauna had been modified by him to a greater or lesser extent. Acceptance of this basic truth then led to fascination for the people who had been in these places before me. Exmoor proved to be a perfect example of this semi-wild country where the tides of mankind had ebbed and flowed for millennia. and because its population had always remained low, the evidence left behind by earlier settlers had rarely been obliterated by later arrivals.

From the outset it was also evident that Exmoor

people were friendly, whether they were natives or incomers, and many of the latter proved to be like-minded outdoor people. Other advantages include a relatively mild climate, reasonable access to other parts of the country and an absence of crowds even at the height of the summer.

Having made a provisional decision to move to Exmoor, it was necessary to become more familiar with the region and to this end we bought a small holiday home. All our earlier impressions were subsequently reinforced and the decision became a firm one. It was a course of action that we have never regretted.

CHAPTER NINETEEN

ACROSS ENGLAND
THE START TO MARKET
HARBOROUGH

On approaching retirement my wish to walk in new scenes had to some extent been replaced by a need to renew acquaintance with old ones. Some return visits had been disappointing and I wanted to check whether other happy memories might now have too rosy a glow. It must be said that many recent sightings of the English countryside from motorways and railways had been far from encouraging.

The major lifestyle change with retirement meant that there would be more time for walking. During the lead up period, my mind ranged pleasurably over possible projects. One of these was to walk from the region where I had been born to the one where I would live in retirement and by the time retirement came this idea had crystallised into a concrete plan. Initially, I had hoped that my journey from Gibraltar Point to Minehead's North Hill would include some of my much-loved northern hills, but this proved impractical because the length of the walk, even heading across the Midlands, was already in excess of five hundred miles. I reconciled this shortcoming with the thought that although much of my adult life had been spent hankering after the uplands in reality, by birth, upbringing and residence, most of my life to date belonged to the lowlands. However, as consolation I promised myself an excursion around Exmoor's uplands at the end. The proposed journey would not be a marathon. In deference to age and ability, I planned to walk for one week out of four during the spring and summer months of 1992, with each stage approximately one hundred miles in length.

So, on an unpromising grey spring morning, my dreams and plans finally became reality as I travelled up by train from King's Cross to Skegness. Alighting from the carriage at the destination, with my bulky new rucksack suspended unbalanced from one shoulder, I staggered and nearly fell. This ineptitude caused a long moment of hesitation as I stood on the wet platform. All previous enthusiasm had suddenly drained away and the task that I had set myself now seemed to be of mammoth proportions. Then a taxi sped me through the streets of a seaside resort preparing for the new summer season and stopped beside the deserted Nature Reserve Visitor Centre at Gibraltar Point. By now rain was streaming down.

However, once underway, the world seemed an altogether better place. I walked out beside the muddy Steeping River to the sea bank facing the Wash. I had chosen this spot as my starting point, rather than my home village some ten miles to the north, because it was an immediately recognisable map feature. But here there was no sea or land, only dark brown flats fading into distant haze. But above the wind, waves could be heard breaking on a shore somewhere to the north and I headed off towards them. With wind and rain comfortably on my back, I wandered through a wilderness where stretches of sand and mud alternated with brackish pools and creeks, and where bushes and bramble covered dunes hid everything else on the landward side.

The sound of the sea grew louder until, in one of those quick scene changes familiar to walkers, I suddenly found myself on the sea front at Skegness. From here, and for the next twenty miles, the sea was very much in evidence along a very vulnerable stretch of coast. The top of a new mighty concrete sea wall led to my home village of Chapel St. Leonards for the first overnight stop. The guest house was one of the few dwellings in the village which had a view over the sea and had been the home of an old sea captain when I was young. Before retiring, I peered from my bedroom window for a last look around. On one side I could sense the unchanging growling mass of dark waters and, on the other, see a myriad of street lights where few had been in my childhood.

The next morning's weather was cool, breezy and sunny. Beyond Chapel Point all other humanity had gone and my journey became a delight with a shining sea on my right, lonely sand dunes covered by marram grass and buckthorn on my left, and pebble strewn golden sands stretching ahead as a highway. Waves rushed and retreated at my feet as the sun warmed and the wind cooled my back. Successions of seagulls, resting on diminishing strips of sand as the tide came in, flew away in raucous complaint on my approach. At intervals I climbed the dunes to peer inland. Beyond a reedy strip of marsh separating the coast from the grassy 'Roman' Bank, lonely pasture and arable land stretched away towards the distant hazy Wolds. The big sea wall and motley buildings of Mablethorpe came next, the sky became overcast, the air cool, the beach broad and extensive landward dunes returned. The last of Mablethorpe was a lone fisherman standing on the edge of the distant sea and after that there was nobody until arriving at Saltfleet for the night. Out of season Saltfeet also seemed near deserted until a noisy party at the pub continued into the early hours. Next morning I walked along a lonely coast of marshes, sand dunes, and broad shores to Cleethorpes.

Then there were two days of wandering through a mainly industrial scene along the Humber Bank, with stops at Immingham and Barton upon Humber. Beyond the last I turned my back on England's eastern sea and joined the Viking Way. Its first stage led me along the length of the Lincolnshire Wolds with their wide prairies, few trees, minimal hedges and isolated buildings. I met fewer than ten people in this countryside over the next thirty miles and three of them were young lads whom I overtook at a nameless spot. Burdened by camping equipment and with bottles banging awkwardly against bare legs, their progress was slow. They told me that they were aiming for Grasby that night and for distant Biscathorpe on the next. I did not see them again and later wondered whether they had reached their goals. On the following morning near Walesby, a lone walker approached at high speed and suddenly stopped beside me. He was the current Guinness Book's Endurance Walk Record Holder out on a practise march. Somewhat incongruously in all that empty space, Ron H. Bullen suddenly delved into one of his many pockets, gave a formal bow and, with a flourish, presented me with one of his personal cards. Later, at a field corner near the all-but abandoned Walesby Church, I found two sapling oaks planted in memory of my old friend Nev Cole. We had come this way together sixteen years before.

Beyond a long abandoned RAF airfield, the Way petered out to a track not far from the sunken roadways and house platforms of the deserted villages of East and West Wykeham. Nearby, but out of sight, there were also those of North Cadeby, South Cadeby and Calcethorpe. These villages,located on relatively poor soils, dwindled and died after the climate deteriorated in the Middle Ages and the undernourished inhabitants became an easy prey for disease. The settlements had existed for at least five centuries and by now had been dead for as long again, but a persistent aura of human failure still haunted the solitude of these empty hills.

Large fields rolled gently away on all sides, sometimes green with growing crops and elsewhere white where the bones of chalk showed through. There were no signs of any present day human activity, but Grims Mound, a Bronze Age tomb with a much younger Scandinavian name, eventually came into view with white scars where modern plough discs had cut deep into its sides. Biscathorpe, a former village, was now reduced to a rare green pasture, a single house and a small decorated Victorian Gothick church. The final stretch of that day's walk beside the River Bain led to a very quiet Donington on a Sunday evening. Although the weather remained bright, the air by now had become bitterly cold.

Next day I walked in the wet along a twisting route which nowadays was well sign-posted and provided with foot bridges across the intervening becks. Things had been very different when Nev and I first came along here in 1976. The Way had then been difficult to find, especially as the new signposts had already been uprooted and many removed. In Goulceby, we had been hooted and sworn at by a crowd of youngsters who nevertheless kept themselves at a safe distance. Now the village appeared quiet and orderly with brand new properties redolent of London suburbia.

After two days spent wandering along these slow rolling chalk hills, the top of a rise suddenly revealed the immense level Fenland plain ahead. With the improving weather, fluffy white clouds created a vast slow moving chequerboard of sunlight and shade. And that was not all. Lincoln Cathedral, distantly visible for the past two days, was now much closer and I planned to reach it on the afternoon of the next day. Horncastle, a small town of Roman origin, was once famous throughout Europe for its annual horse fair. As I walked through not one of these creatures was anywhere in sight, a potent sign of how much farming has changed in recent times. I then joined the Spa Trail which followed the route of an old railway to Woodhall Spa. The surroundings had now become very sandy and, in spite of overnight rain, dust was being whipped high into the sky by the wind. At this early season, new crop growth was not yet sufficient to bind the soil, a problem exacerbated locally by the modern day absence of hedges.

Woodhall Spa was completely different, a small modern settlement set on a heath in the middle of Lincolnshire's immense intensive farmland which resembled a suburb in the sandy Surrey commuter belt.

The next day was very dull, wet and windy. At Bergamoor the Way passed between two fields crowded with hundreds of sheep and their lambs. Stepping gingerly through this mass, I was anxious not to disturb them and at first all went well. Then a lone animal gave a short bleat and within seconds all of them were at it. This cacophony in a previously silent countryside had a shattering effect on me. Acutely embarrassed at being the cause of all the upheaval, I hurried away as quickly as possible.

From there I tramped on through an empty rain soaked countryside. On occasionally stopping, the otherwise constant rustle of my rain gear and creak of my rucksack ceased, leaving a world of profound silence apart from gently dripping water. Humans were absent for several bleak miles, and then I was pleased to see a lone figure ahead, at work with a fork in a covered crew yard containing a dubious mix of cattle dung and straw. On approach his dress seemed to introduce some levity into an otherwise very dour day, for he was wearing what once might have been a brass band man's uniform lavishly decorated with gold ribbons, albeit now dirty and torn.

Eagerly anticipating a friendly encounter I wished him a cheery 'Good day', but all I got in return was a short surly response.

'It's better where I am.'

With that rebuff I instinctively let my momentum carry me on and away while a sour thought simultaneously passed through my mind. With his present rate of progress with only a fork in hand, there would be much rain and shine to come before he finished his stinking, mucky task.

The lonely miles continued on to Bardney, once famous for its large abbey, which is now reduced to a few scanty remains, and for its present day huge beet sugar factory. I was now in the Fens, or to be precise, a narrow part of them which extends up the River Witham to Lincoln. This bleak new scene was composed of three unrelieved components, long, straight, grassy embankments beside the river, a sombre fallow plain of dark brown peat stretching into hazy distance and finally a uniform wet, dark grey sky above. And that was not the sum total of unpleasantness. I now had to trudge along an exposed bank straight into a streaming wet wind. But at least my goal in the form of Lincoln Cathedral could be seen in outline above the horizon directly ahead. This end-on silhouette, at once unfamiliar and ungainly, also struck a chord of unpleasant memory. Then it suddenly sprang to mind as the shape of an overly ornate communist building in Eastern Europe. Oh Saints Hugh, both Great and Small, I do hope you forgave me for that fleeting sacrilegious thought!

The gradual narrowing of the Fens provided encouragement to hasten on. Finally, it reduced to the width of a single field near Lincoln. I am fond of this city, but on this occasion, dragged down by soaking clothing, my only interest was in getting home. My luck was in and within a quarter of an hour I was seated in a train heading for Newark, with weary leg muscles tingling gently and a wet body and clothes steaming gently in the warmth of the railway carriage.

A month later, I was heading south along the Lincoln

Cliff, a narrow, limestone ridge with the combined Trent and Witham plain on the west and the Fens on the east. To the south it would eventually widen out to the magical Highlands of my youth before continuing down to Bath. I was to encounter this ridge several times on my way across England. In the present cold weather, only occasional distant patches of yellow rape confirmed the true season. I ate my sandwiches in a small recreation ground at Waddington where the desultory sounds of village life were periodically drowned by deafening jet engine noise from the nearby RAF airfield.

A line of old stone-built villages with lovely churches led me to Wellingore where the Viking Way turned up the Cliff and joined Ermine Street, the old Roman main road to the north, nowadays in the form of a straight track with cowslips blooming along its broad verges. All the while the wind's constant roar could never quite drown the continuing song of skylarks. The remains of the Templars' Temple Bruer were passed by before reaching the isolated spot known as Byards Leap, where I spent the night. According to local legend, Byard was a horse who was accidentally killed as his master was dispatching a particularly nasty local witch by the name of Meg. By way of confirmation, some extremely large iron horse shoes lay in the long grass close to my overnight lodgings, but they proved to be romantic nineteenth century additions.

Next morning, the route soon turned away from both Ermine Street and a wearisome head wind. Large fields of deep green cereals now stretched away on every side. Apart from one difference, I might well have been back on the empty Wolds of a month before. But now a stone wall snaked along by my side, its original brown stones long since greyed by weathering and whitened by lichen. From the Cliff scarp I eventually headed down into a region where scattered villages revealed more signs of humanity.

The Vale of Belvoir may have been pleasant countryside, but I felt that it hardly lived up to the superlative of its Norman French name.

Throughout my journey, few elderly ladies out exercising their dogs in lonely places gave any indication of wishing to engage me in conversation, but here there were two in quick succession.

Without any prompting, the first approached and announced,'I came up here from the South six years ago to be near my son's family. Now they are leaving and so will I.— I don't like this part of the country because the wind blows at Force Ten all the time.'

The wind that morning was particularly cool and fresh so I could appreciate her objection.

The second lady was a seasoned native and therefore had nothing to say about the weather, but she in turn wanted to bend my ear on another matter.

'I come onto the Viking Way every day because it is well known and does not give farmers any opportunity to complain at my presence. On other paths I have to put up with frequent unpleasant confrontations.'

Saddened to hear this after my so far trouble-free passage, I privately wondered whether this lady might have been picked on because she was a woman.

Wishing them both well in turn, I continued on. Crossing under the main line from Kings Cross by means of an underpass was easy and safe, but that over the very busy A1 was difficult and dangerous.

The next village, Allington, had a nowadays rare village shop, so I stopped to purchase a soft drink. The relaxed owner obviously welcomed a chat with anyone passing by. Having said that he saw few walkers, the man then went on to give details of two men who had arrived at his shop crippled with bad blisters. Taking pity on their miserable condition, he had given them a lift in his car to their next overnight lodgings which, turned out to be mine as well. From his detailed description, I gained the impression that the event had taken place recently. However, on signing the visitors book next morning, I noticed that it had been over six months before. Clearly, little happened in this quiet corner of England.

The lady of the house was a lonely widow. Long into the evening she talked about her life and that of her late husband. I also learnt that the house was considered to be haunted and so was shunned by local people. In any case, from the surrounding empty scene on arrival there did not seem to be many of them either. The building had apparently been the local isolation hospital and the ghost was said to be that of a mischievous young girl who had died of a fever. This spirit was also said to move objects around inside the house and could often be seen out in the garden wearing a long dress or coat. The next morning was fine and sunny, but before taking a close look at the weather, I sheepishly scrutinised the garden for the girl's presence.

The Viking Way now joined Sewstern Drift, a broad track parallel to the Great North Road (the present A1), and this continued for many miles to the south. Its great age was evident from the fact that it had long been the boundary between Lincolnshire and neighbouring Leicestershire. In previous centuries it had also been used as an alternative to the nearby Great North Road by cattle drovers on the way to London thereby avoiding toll payments on their herds.

On the previous day, bulky Belvoir Castle had caught my eye, a large castle-like country house. Its strategic position suggested that a former genuine stronghold had once stood on the same site. This prominent feature now dropped to the rear as the Drift climbed onto a low plateau where the air was cooler and crops less advanced. The nearby views were always changing, but the haunting, taunting, spring call of the cuckoo never went away. Sometimes, happy crowds of cowslips peeped from the grass verges and, elsewhere, shy bluebells formed deep blue pools beneath wayside coppices and woods. It was the first time during my walk that I seemed to be heading towards summer and the south and I revelled in the thought.

I knew Saltby Airfield was not far away, but even so the sight of a distant glider apparently crossing the track ahead came as a surprise. The reason was soon obvious. The main runway of a wartime airfield had been built across the Drift and this had now been acquired by a gliding club. However, on closer examination, I wondered whether 'gliding club' was a true description for although these aircraft looked the part with their long slim wings and bodies, they were also equipped with small engines and propellers.

On stopping to pass the time of day with a man who was pottering with one of these engines, he told me that an elderly American tourist, who had been based here as a Hamilcar glider pilot during the Second World War, had recently returned to the site. Apparently disappointed on failing to recognise any of his surroundings, this veteran had persuaded my new companion to take him aloft, from where he was able to identify the once familiar countryside and also became extremely excited. In response I told him that I had once been here in rather different circumstances. By 1952 flying had ceased, but during one day and one night, my RAF colleagues and I had defended the airfield against a mock enemy attack. It had been a lovely spring day, like the one at present, and we had basked in the warm sun for the first time after a hard winter. The following night and its attack was an altogether different matter. Mindful that there was still a long way to go that day, I brought our conversation to an end. Out of sight around a corner, a lady, presumably the man's wife, had sat quietly knitting at the door of a small caravan throughout our long chat.

Along the way I passed by, but did not identify, the spot where Rutland, Leicestershire and Lincolnshire came together. It was here that I finally said goodbye to my home county after walking up and down its length for nearly two hundred miles. This triangular boundary point became notorious in 1811 as the site of an illegal boxing match between Tom Cribb, the British champion, and Tom Molineux, the challenger. The venue was chosen in case up to two of the three county authorities decided to ban the match. The fight did go ahead and by all accounts was an infamous bloody affair.

Footsore and hot, I trudged into the village of Exton basking in the mellow sunshine of late afternoon. Its warm stone cottages, roofed in both stone and thatch, made it the most beautiful village that I had encountered so far. That evening I took a gentle stroll away from the centre of the village to the romantic ruined Old Hall and adjacent impressive village church. Only one inhabited dwelling stood beside the latter and as insects danced in the still air and shadows lengthened, I suddenly became aware of something that I had not noticed before. Bumps in the adjacent pasture had regular forms. Then I knew that the village had once been up here beside the church. Across the country from the late Middle Ages onwards, rich landowners had built new mansions for themselves. If nearby villages were considered to be unsightly or to obstruct the view, then they were often summarily removed. If this had happened here, then the villagers were at least provided with alternative accommodation. In many other cases they were simply thrown out of their homes and that was the end of it.

Beyond Exton, the Viking Way continued along

roads, passing impressive Rutland Water on the way to its end in the small unspoilt Midland town of Oakham. From here to the West Midlands there were no suitable long distance paths to follow and I now had to pick my way along public rights of way shown on maps or to follow canal towpaths. In practice I used a combination of both.

The afternoon became very hot and, as I passed through a succession of stone villages, all attractive, but none quite matching the exceptional beauty of Exton, I began to wilt. Towards the end of that day's walk both head and stomach aches developed. Following the example of surrounding sheep, all I now wanted was to lie down in the shade of a tree or bush and close my eyes. After being unable to eat my meal that evening, I began to vomit and this was followed by an uncomfortable sleepless night before the pain finally eased towards dawn.

Rugby had been my goal, but that was no longer possible in my weakened condition, especially as the new day again promised to be hot. So instead I chose to wander to nearby Market Harborough and catch a train to St. Pancras.

My overnight accommodation stood on the edge of the flat flood plain of the upper River Welland. Feeling fragile, I cautiously walked along the line of an obviously disused bridleway. One of the fields contained a herd of bullocks and another cows with their calves. Being unable to run in my poor state, I hoped that this was not going to be a day for animal problems. Very tentatively I stepped through both groups of beasts in turn without giving any of them the least concern or, for that matter, receiving any recognition. Later, I crossed the infant River Welland, here a meandering stream of clear water bounded by waving reeds, grassy banks and green pastures, very different from the unpleasant river which I had known in my youth at Spalding.

Moving along a very quiet country lane, I passed a long succession of hedges smothered in white May blossom at its peak of perfection. At the same time, lines of distant green hills marched slowly past to the rear. Here, in the very heart of England, a great peace prevailed. Although this was only one of many beautiful scenes so far encountered, on this particular morning, perhaps due to my weakened condition, I was momentarily overcome by the splendour of it all and tears welled up into my eyes.

On arriving in a quiet, leafy suburb of Market Harborough, I sat down on a seat for a while to recoup my limited strength. As previously in the countryside, there was little activity and the station too was somnolent until the train arrived. I had looked forward to viewing the countryside in its early summer garb as we sped southwards, but a wave of weariness swept over me as the train pulled out of the station and I fell fast asleep.

CHAPTER TWENTY

ACROSS ENGLAND
MARKET HARBOROUGH TO
CHELTENHAM

It was now June and the day promised to be hot. Already, the part of my back covered by the rucksack was wet with perspiration only a few steps away from Market Harborough Station. I was now heading for England's narrowboat canal system on the outskirts of the town. Hopefully, this would avoid way-finding problems, as I was about to cross part of the Industrial Midlands between Market Harborough and the Cotswolds. From previous map study, this did not appear to be promising walking country.

The towpath of the Market Harborough Canal proved to be covered with long grass, soaking wet from heavy overnight dew, which soon penetrated my socks, trousers and boots. However, there was compensation in this damp because it retained the cool of the previous night. The waterway then twisted and turned along the side of a headwater tributary of the River Welland, presenting wide views over a landscape of growing crops. Nearby, cream elderberry sprays were in bloom, lily flags splashed yellow along the water margins and honeysuckle, with its exquisite scent, dangled across my path. Best of all were the wild roses with delicate petals like the fresh skin of young girls, ranging from white to blushing pink.

The first section of the waterway was little used by

either boats or towpath wanderers, but the canal junction and locks at Foxton were vibrant with human activity and colourful boats. Even the waterside path became a neat gritted track, but only for a short distance before peaceful surroundings and the overgrown path again returned. Although occasional pleasure boats now chugged past, few pedestrians obviously came this way. The new season's lush growth made the going heavy and slow and more than once I just managed to avoid falling into the water where collapsed sections of path were hidden by dense, long grass. A hot sun was beating down from on high by the time I reached Husbands Bosworth and by now all the world seemed to have come to a halt apart from myself. Before eating lunch on a seat shaded by a tall brick wall close to the village centre, I removed my squelching dew-soaked boots and squeezed as much water as possible from my socks before hanging them out to dry in the hot sun.

Periodically, inhabitants slid past, viewing me openly from a distance, but always lowering or averting their eyes on approach. Few returned my greetings, very different from the reaction of local people on earlier stages of the walk. At the time I put this change down to the fact that I had now moved from rural to semi-urban England, but whether this was the case I do not know.

Although Husbands Bosworth was neither prepossessing or welcoming, it did mark a very important milestone on my journey. For here was the watershed of England. Had the map not alerted me, this feature might well have gone unnoticed, but close scrutiny of the surroundings revealed that the ground dropped away gradually to both front and rear. From this point onwards rivers and streams would no longer flow to the north and east, but to the south and west.

I returned from the village to the canal where the world, now bathed in great heat, was still and almost silent. For minutes on end rare gentle chirrups from birds in nearby bushes and occasional water splashes from fishes were all that interrupted a persistent distant hum of insects. Blue dragonflies darted silently along the fringes of the water, and apart from them there was no movement all the way out to the far horizon. I had come this way to avoid industrial conurbations and towns and to my great surprise had found a world of total peace.

Yelvertoft's name struck a chord of memory. Most place names of either total or part Danish origin had been left behind many miles to the rear and yet one existed here. At some point in the tenth or eleventh centuries this would have been one of their most westerly outposts. I purchased a cool drink and an ice-cream from the village shop and flopped down on the shady concrete apron in front of it to enjoy both. Crick, where I stayed that night, proved more attractive than Husbands Bosworth in spite of the constant hum of traffic on the nearby M1 Motorway.

Next morning, a bridleway led down to an underpass beneath this noisy traffic artery. Entry to it brought a sudden pleasing hush in the loud traffic roar and, at the same time, alerted me to an unexpected problem. The surface of the underpass was under water. It seemed that the high engineering standards applied to the highway above did not extend to this secondary way below. By hugging the wall and moving forward slowly a step at a time, I managed to pass through without any water of dubious purity overtopping my boots. Relief on emerging unscathed was immediately replaced by confrontation with a similar, but even more unpleasant challenge. Another underpass, this one beneath the main railway line between London and the Midlands, was not only filled by a pool of green turbid water, but was also occupied by a herd of bullocks! They poked inquisitively at me and my rucksack as I inched forward along an insecure fence bounding the mire, and at one point one of them impudently urinated on a spot where I was about to tread. Fortunately, the firm ground ahead had a covering of dew-wet long grass on which to clean my boots.

In between these two underpass incidents I had passed another important milestone on my long journey, one that provided reminders of two separate periods of England's history. The undistinguished track sandwiched between the M1 and the mainline railway had once been Watling Street, the main Roman road between Londinium and the North West. Then six, hundred years after the Romans had departed, it became the boundary between the Danelaw and the surviving Anglo-Saxon kingdoms. Paradoxically, beyond this frontier I then came across a cluster of places with Danish names. Kilsby, Barby and Willoughby lay on my route, Nortoft and Danetre were nearby and not far away the outskirts of Rugby were heating up in the morning sun. From here on there were to be no more of these names along the way.

Apart from the place name changes, another marked difference between the East and West Midlands soon became apparent. So far on my journey all the local accents had been ones which I could relate to. On the following day there was no detectable accent at Leamington Spa, but on the next when I arrived at Alcester, tired and sticky after struggling through a dense forest of broad beans, I encountered a West Country burr for the first time. In addition, up to Crick everyone had either visited or been aware of my starting point at Gibraltar Point, but after that it was unknown.

Beyond Watling Street, the Oxford Canal towpath proved to be far too dilapidated to walk along and I was obliged to follow lanes between scattered villages. The landscape here was wide and slow rolling, with few trees and large farms. All around, the green wheat was beginning to turn to light gold. With little shade from the sun, the heat of the day became oppressive in spite of an intermittent cool breeze. Near Willoughby, the last Danish named village, I encountered the sad remains of the old Great Central Railway which once had a splendid fast track and very few level crossings. A former main line connecting London with Leicester, Nottingham, Sheffield and Manchester, its through services were terminated in the 1960s, a loss which the nation may well have cause to regret as modern transport problems multiply. Later, at Long Itchington, I joined the Grand Union Canal and followed its well maintained towpath to Leamington Spa.

Next day, the same canal took me westwards to a point where I joined the Heart of England Way. Having, as I thought, said goodbye to the canal system which had served me well from Market Harborough onwards, but whose scenery had of late become rather boring, I immediately became involved with the narrow branch waterway heading for Stratford-on-Avon. With time to spare on that day's short walk, I allowed these surroundings to ensnare me. Sitting down on the warm sheltered greensward beside a lock, I removed my boots and socks, used my rucksack as a pillow and immediately fell asleep, only be wakened by the clatter of lock operation each time a boat passed through. Finally, much refreshed, I continued on to my night's lodgings.

The next day's walk was long and tiring. Beyond Henley-in-Arden and the imposing site of its once large castle, I found myself among rolling hills covered with a mix of growing wheat, pastures and woodland, with each combination forming constantly changing pleasant views. The surprise when it came was sudden. Rounding a corner at Banhams Wood, I looked up to find a wide panorama ahead. Just at that moment the sun chose to appear for the first time that day. Behind me were the green slopes which

I had just crossed. To the south blue hills stretched away behind outliers of the Cotswolds, where later that day I was to rejoin the Jurassic limestone ridge after a long break. However, it was the western scene which commanded most attention because here a bumpy outline of ancient rocks marked the boundary between Lowland and Upland Britain. Included among the latter was the miniature mountain range of the Malverns. At the time I thought that there would be many more opportunities to admire them, but, in the event, the weather dictated othewise. Between me and these delectable features there was a hidden trench which marked the Vale of Severn, a feature which was to be my constant companion during the days ahead.

The Heart of England Way had been little used in recent times and consequently was often overgrown. This slowed my rate of progress and, with time pressing, by the second half of the afternoon I was obliged to abandon the path and follow roads. My recollections of this final stage are all disagreeable and include speeding traffic, massive storage sheds, a large bleak housing estate, a dull sky, increasing chill in the air and, worst of all, painful feet brought about by pounding on the hard road surfaces. Then, at Upper Quinton, I finally found something to my liking in the form of prominent Meon Hill standing at the northern end of the Cotswolds.

Later, I strolled down to the pub at the lower end of the village for my evening meal. Initially all was peaceful, but just as my food had been placed before me and I was literally about to take my first bite, a bus load of American tourists swarmed in. First they blocked out nearly all the light from the windows and then they conducted a series of drawling shouting matches over my head. They seemed to be nice people, but how I wished that they were not there. From overheard exchanges I gathered that on previous days they had done Ireland, Wales and Scartland and had now come to this village to look at the church and some birds before a night in Stratford and a return to Ohio on the morrow. On leaving the pub it seemed worthwhile taking a second look at the church. It was an elegant building, but I was far too tired to take the matter any further.

When I commented to my landlady that Meon Hill was attractive, she agreed, but added that it was considered to be haunted and also that someone had once been impaled to the ground by a pitchfork after being murdered there. At first I thought that the crime might have been committed long ago, but then my memory was stirred and I recalled reading something about it in a newspaper many years before. Subsequent research reminded me that the body of a farm worker had been found on the hill in 1945, not only with its throat cut, but also transfixed to the ground with a pitchfork. It appeared that executed witches were once impaled in this fashion to prevent them walking away after death. This 1945 mystery was never solved and perhaps the evil influences were still at work, for on the following morning I temporarily lost my way on Meon Hill.

The golden brown buildings at the centre of Mickleton announced my entry to the Cotswold scene. From here I climbed the steep scarp slope of the Jurassic Ridge for the first time since leaving it behind at Carlton Scroop in Lincolnshire. This broad swath of rock extends across the centre of England from the coast of North Yorkshire to the Dorset seaside and in prehistoric times provided a trade route across the heart of the country. Its characteristic stone, widely used for buildings and field walls, creates a scene which many foreigners consider as quintessentially English, but is in fact only one of many different types of rustic architecture found in this country.

Footpaths now showed signs of regular use and for the

very first time on my walk I encountered a group of ramblers. Chipping Camden was still the old golden town remembered from twenty years before, but nearby Dover's Hill was cold and uncomfortable with all distant views obscured by grey dismal haze. On the path leading from Broadway Tower down to Broadway, a warm sun at last broke through the grey. Then the Cotswold Way headed back up to lovely high places where sheep grazed, colourful wild flowers grew in profusion and hazy blue hills shimmered in the middle distance. After that the route dropped down along a shady grassy glade before a final long slow slog up to Stumps Cross, one climb too many on a hot afternoon.

At the top, open space and a cooling breeze provided a reward. An uneven green skyline set against a blue sky marked Beckbury Fort on the edge of the scarp, with its enclosing ditch and bank still impressive after well over two thousand years of weathering. Further along, I came across a curious stone feature composed of a carved pillar attached to a flat projection. With my curiosity aroused, I resolved to make some enquiries about it at my next overnight stop in Hailes.

Finally, a gentle downhill track, with trees and bushes on one side and a very large apple orchard on the other, led me down to this hamlet. The dappled shade and increasing cool of late afternoon brought welcome relief after the heat of recent hours. Muted pleasurable sounds came from nearby insects, birds chirping in the undergrowth and, most unusually, from the music of a distant radio. At the bottom, the new scene was in concert with the mellow warmth and consisted of the minimal but attractive remains of the abbey, an intact rustic parish church, an old tree-lined meadow with the remains of a preaching cross at its centre and stone cottages surrounded by scented flower gardens.

The house where I spent the night was on the site of a former pilgrims' hostel and many of its stones and timbers were said to have been incorporated into the present structure. Hailes had once been a place of pilgrimage for its phial said to contain a sample of Christ's blood. At dissolution, this relic was removed to London for analysis and, presumably to the satisfaction of the new national church, was found to contain honey coloured with saffron.

The much depleted abbey remains intrigued me so I rose early next morning to take a look. At this dewy time on a grey morning, considerable numbers of wild rabbits were busily nibbling the well tended lawns and paying scant regard to me. Apart from a few graceful arches and some dwarf stone walls, little remained of this once substantial establishment. I also wandered over to the nearby parish church. Although of simple design and constructed of random stonework, it had changed little over the years. The building was locked, but I did manage to glimpse a startling medieval wall painting within.

My enquiries about the curious stone feature at the top of the hill yielded a mix of fact, conjecture and fiction. It was said that the stone feature had been the seat from which Cromwell had watched the sacking of Hailes Abbey, the clear inference being that the man in question was Oliver Cromwell. However, dissolution of the monasteries had taken place well before his time and had been carried out by Thomas Cromwell (no relation) who had been King Henry the VIII's treasurer. In reality the dissolution of Hailes appears to have been a relatively, peaceful affair with both the abbot and monks being given the medieval equivalent of redundancy. What took place next was not. As at many other similar monastic sites across the country, the beautiful abbey buildings were sold off to a contractor who demolished them and then retailed reusable stones for nearby building work. Local legends often place the blame on Oliver Cromwell for this type of desecration and I believe that they came about because later generations, now concerned with what they saw, tried to place the blame elsewhere.

I did not keep an accurate record of the miles covered on my journey, but around the middle of the preceding day I had passed the three hundred miles mark from Gibraltar Point. From the outset I was determined to walk every single step of the way and consequently offers of lifts, which often came at the most surprising times and places, all had to be politely declined.

Quiet wheat fields stood along the foot of the hills to Winchcombe, once a seat of Mercian rulers. Then another familiar Cotswold hill climb led me to a part of the ridge crowned by the long barrow known as Belas Knap. Before modern trees intervened, this four thousand years old structure would have dominated the hill basin around Winchcombe. After examining and then pondering on the tomb for some time, I wondered whether its long survival had depended on the fear it had engendered over many generations. Having seen nobody for some miles, and with the atmosphere that morning silent and brooding under a very dull sky, I sensed that the aura of sadness here also contained a hint of threat.

The wind blowing across the open tops was now surprisingly chill. The nearby linseed and rape crops were late, still in full flower when elsewhere their Mediterranean blues and sunshine yellows had gone leaving only straggly stems and oily seed pods behind. The Way then ran beside rough limestone walls and fields of cereals, a reminder of similar scenes a hundred and fifty miles back along the way, but a marked change was soon to come. A long stone wall appeared ahead and a gate in it led onto a wide gorsey, grassy moor heading towards Cleeve Hill. At long last my journey had provided me with a reminder of all those delightful heaths and moors which I have loved so much over the years, but nowadays are rare in Lowland England.

So far, this morning, I had only encountered one person in the countryside, but after crossing a deep combe enshrouded in hazy gloom, I suddenly found myself surrounded by golfers, model aeroplane fliers, horse riders, doggy walkers and many others with no observable activity. I had now arrived on the top of famous Cleeve Hill. As often on my journey the sun came out on cue, but unfortunately this time it only highlighted hazy views of an urban sprawl far below.

I turned away southwards, following the scarp. Although human numbers gradually declined, the golf course and its denizens seemed determined to remain with me for as long as possible. A confusing maze of paths along the top gradually reduced to a single one and, after finally encountering a man and his dog, nobody else remained but myself. Alone and in total peace, I sat on the sunny grassy hillside, resting, drinking and eating. The view over the Severn Vale was still as hazy as ever, but the weaving western outline of the Cotswolds continued for some distance southwards before finally disappearing. Those hills were not for me on that day. After heading down the first road down to Cheltenham, I phoned from a wayside phone box for a luxurious taxi ride to the town's railway station.

CHAPTER TWENTY ONE

ACROSS ENGLAND
CHELTENHAM TO CHEDDAR

Even the best laid plans can go awry. As mentioned earlier, my original intention had been to walk for one week out of every four during spring and summer months and I was able to stick to this schedule as far as Cheltenham. Then, metaphorically, I became stuck in that town for two months. After a year on the market, our home in Northwood was sold with surprising speed and, for the next two months, my wife and I were totally preoccupied with our move to Minehead. Following this unexpected delay, my walk now had an added incentive, for every step along the way would take me towards our new home.

It was already late summer when my wife brought me back to Cheltenham. The advanced season was evident in a mellowing sun, cooler evenings and chilly nights. On setting out, there were more signs of change by the wayside in the form of fluffed-out thistle parachutes ready to fly and collections of dazzling, orange-red berries hanging from occasional rowans. Sadly, my lovely wild roses, the constant companions of earlier stages, had now all gone. Out on the slow rolling farmland of the tops beyond the Cotswold ridge, some harvesting was still underway, but many fields had already been turned over by the plough. The work was being carried out by noisy machinery, so not only were my roses gone, but so was the former almost universal peace of the countryside.

The one thing that had not changed in the interim was a persistent haze hiding all distant views over the Vale of Severn. The Cotswold Way now began to dodge to and fro, following the irregular ups and downs of the broken hill scarp. This caused me frustration because the massed buildings of Cheltenham simply refused to fall behind for a long time. The late holiday season was still evident from the crowds at Crickley Hill Country Park and busy main roads which often proved difficult to cross. Until mid-afternoon, the day had failed to bring back the peaceful enjoyment of earlier stages, but this finally returned on escaping down a quiet track through extensive woodland on the way to my overnight stop at Coopers Hill.

The tea garden, where I stayed, was basically an extended wooden hut, serving as a reminder of my first rambling days when hutted tea places, although declining in numbers, still proved popular focal points for rambles.

The next morning was cool, gloomy and, as usual, very hazy, but on this occasion rain was also clearly in the offing. The unique fame of Coopers Hill had been brought to my attention the previous evening and, on setting out, I took a look at the course of the Spring Bank Holiday annual cheese race. I believe a wooden disc has now replaced the original cheese chased downhill by a crowd of runners. My first reaction to the very steep course was one of wonderment and the second concern, for the injuries sustained by contestants whose momentum carried them forward faster than their legs could carry them.

A long solitary walk through a stately beech forest brought me to a golf course imposed on the beauty spot of Painswick Hill. Painswick itself turned out to be a former small market town built of amazing silver white stone, but even this failed to ameliorate the increasing gloom of the day.

Drizzle began while I stood admiring the elegant

parish church and its well shorn yew trees but, choosing to ignore it, I continued on with my rain gear still stowed away. Then, while crossing the abandoned quarry on Scotsquar Hill, the rain suddenly descended with intent and I quickly donned all my protective gear. It was the first occasion that I had done so since the wet, windy day in May while approaching Lincoln along the exposed Fenland bank. Now I was to some extent sheltered by the surrounding leafy woodland and, enclosed within my personal cocoon, the world became a very tiny one, where only the noise of my footsteps, the rustle of rain gear and the constant creak of my rucksack made any impression. Thus, few external features captured my attention. But one of the few that did was a monument commemorating the Royalist relief of Gloucester in 1643, nowadays paradoxically known as Cromwell's Stone.

From Haresfield Beacon, a magnificent promontory crowned by an Iron Age fort, there were no views whatsoever through the wet haze. So the special feature which my eyes sought was not there to see. Then a long trek led me through dark stretches of Ruscombe Woods with never another person in sight. Finally, as the surrounding scene became more open, the rain petered out. A hazy sun now penetrated through the clouds to reveal lower ground and the misty silhouettes of buildings ahead. I was now entering the Frome Valley, an old industrial area whose prosperity had been based on wool before its factories moved away to the North. Some of the surviving large stone mill buildings, only imperfectly visible on that day, reminded me of ones seen earlier in the north. I spent the night at Kings Stanley, an old village on the opposite side of this former industrial belt. Having expanded when the mills prospered, its buildings were now a mix of old rural stone, Victorian brick with slate and modern miscellanies.

The air of the new day was crisp. Above, woolly white clouds and blue filled the sky while below, my boots left a long wet trail through the dewy grass. Pen Hill, a name which literally means 'Hill Hill', probably arose because the Anglo-Saxons did not understand the meaning of the British word 'Pen'. On briefly emerging from woods it was just possible to discern the outline of distant Welsh Hills but, more importantly, in front of them there was the feature which had been invisible on the preceding day. Now, the upper tidal reaches of the Severn Estuary had come into view as a thin light grey line, marking another significant landmark on my journey across to the Western Sea.

While passing another Neolithic tomb, the sun emerged properly, revealing a panorama of steep, wooded hills ahead. So the intrinsic pleasure of this scene was tempered by realisation that there would be many tiring ups and downs on a day that promised to become hot.

Descending towards Dursley, I encountered the sickening sight of a rabbit in its death throes from disease, but did not have the guts to put it out of its misery. Dursley appeared bright and cheerful although its industry was then already in trouble. From there I made my way up through woods to Stinchcombe Hill, another high promontory above the Vale of Severn crowned by a prominent Iron Age fort which had subsequently been invaded by a golf course. The view from the top was more than worth the effort of the climb. Below, the Severn Estuary twisted away downstream to where the Severn Bridge was just visible through the haze. On the near side of the Severn, an attractive mosaic of green fields and hedges was disrupted by the massive bulk of disused Berkeley nuclear power station, an alien intrusion in the scene destined to remain long into the future. Immediately below the traffic hurtling along the broad noisy M5 was not to be encountered again until the vicinity of Bridgwater. A nearby indicator board pointed out the direction of Dunkery Beacon, Exmoor's highest hill. Although invisible on that day, it provided a comforting reminder that my ultimate goal was no longer very far away.

Steep slopes, alternately wooded and grassy, fell away on my right as the ridge and my route turned eastwards towards Tyndale's Tower, now clearly visible in the distance. By contrast, at my feet tiny brilliant blue butterflies darted among massed small flowers of a similar hue. The impressive feature on top of the next hill was erected during the nineteenth century as a memorial to William Tyndale who at that time was thought to have been born nearby. This great Englishman has now faded from our collective memory, for it was he who first translated the bible into English. Much of his work was later incorporated en bloc into the St. James Bible and it was he who also gave us many phrases and sayings still in common usage, such as 'the salt of the earth', 'the signs of the times', 'eat, drink and be merry' and ' the spirit is willing but the flesh is weak'. As an intellectual rebel and innovator he fell foul of conservative church authorities fearful of losing their authority. During my working years I sometimes went on business to Vilvorde, nowadays a northern suburb of Brussels, and on one trip accidentally discovered that Tyndale was burnt at the stake here in 1536 on the orders of the church hierarchy.

After successive ups and downs, the route, now passing through woodland, levelled out and, together with a good walking surface, speeded my rate of progress. Trees eventually gave way to cereal fields before the Cotswold Way led down to a wind blown clump of trees surrounded by a stone wall. On approach this turned out to be a prominent feature above the small town of Wotton-under-Edge, my destination for the day. I understand that this clump had originally been planted to commemorate the victory at Waterloo, but those trees were consumed in a bonfire marking the end of the Crimean War! Their replacements, the ones currently in view, were planted in 1887. I had now reached the end of the main Cotswold ridge which began at Meon Hill and from here the ground fell away to lower rolling countryside heading southwards towards Bath.

While relaxing on a seat beside the knoll, I fell into conversation with an old gentleman who told me that, although suffering from angina, he regularly came up here two or three times a week. We chatted about the old cloth mills dotted around the countryside below, their positions beside streams indicating that they had originally been water-powered. Some of these buildings had been put to new uses, but others were decayed ruins. My companion then said, with what I thought might have been a hint of bitterness, that the town had never recovered from losing its wool trade and that, as most locals were obliged to go away to find work, it had become a place of old people. Contrary to his assertion, when I reached the town centre it was full of mothers with their young children. My arrival happened to coincide with school leaving time.

A few days later I was back in Wotton with clear signs that the weather was deteriorating. From this point onwards wet and wind were to be my constant companions right up to the end. I climbed out from the pleasantly cool town to the top of the first lower hill ahead. Some late-ripening cereals still remained to be harvested, but nearby hedgerows displayed bedraggled foliage and overripe wild fruits which had slumped in the new chill. Then the Way went down through a deep holloway under arching trees where the grey light of that day all but hid straggling tentacles of ground ivy and limp fronds of ferns fighting to hold on to life. Wet meadows, valleys overhung by woods or medieval lychets and occasional sleepy hamlets followed. Hardly a soul was to be seen anywhere, a very different scene from the popular high Cotswold ridge of previous days and, to be honest, much more to my liking.

Later that morning I passed by the Somerset Monument, dedicated to a man and not to the county of that name, and crossed from Gloucestershire into Avon. My new surroundings of large arable fields with few trees, reminded me of earlier parts of my walk in Lincolnshire. But the seasons had now moved on. The summer's cereals and straw had all been gathered in and most of the fields were bare. At one spot a sudden acrid smell drew my attention to two blackened fields where the straw had been burnt off. It was the only example of this polluting practice that I came across on my journey. Later, pastures and livestock returned to the scene and soon after saying good-day to two lady walkers, the only ones seen that day, the rain began in earnest.

In spite of the wetting and the cocooning effect of rain gear, Little Sodbury Fort attracted my attention because it was large and also had a straight line orderliness not usually associated with Iron Age earthworks. Later, I speculated on whether an Iron Age earthwork might have subsequently been modified and used as Roman fort at the time when the nearby Foss Way served as a temporary frontier of the Roman Empire.

I now had to reconcile myself to a wet trudge dragged down by damp rain gear. My only clear recollection of that part of the journey is of cattle and sheep huddled together with their backs to the weather, immobile but alert watching my every step across their home domains. At length I arrived at the village of Tormarton where, wet, miserable, confused by the poor light and disturbed by noise from the nearby M4, I at first managed to leave the village in the wrong direction! The Tormarton

213

Interchange, between the busy A46 and the even busier M4, was an awful place. As far as I could see in the poor light, there were no paths or any other pedestrian safety features on the roundabout and slip roads. Here, the never ending streams of swishing, spraying vehicles travelling at high speed around bends, the blinding headlights, the interminable noise and the constant mortal danger, all combined to create a man-made hellish maelstrom. Following this, the lay-by on the A46, although busy, was a relatively peaceful haven until my wife came along in our car to pick me up.

Returning the following morning, a Sunday, all was quiet at the lay-by. Beyond the immediate screen of trees, farmland stretched back towards the high ridge of the Cotswolds and Tyndale's Tower. To the west, the distant mass of Bristol was partly hidden by a dark grey cloud moving along and pouring out rain as it went, an ominous sign in view of the day's poor weather forecast. From the boundary of Dyrham Park, Hinton Hill, with an Iron Age fort on its summit and medieval lychet strips cut along its sides, presented a fine sight. Although largely unrecognised today, this hill has a special place in our history for it was here in 577 AD that a decisive battle took place between the Anglo-Saxons and the native Britons. The Anglo-Saxon invasion of Britain, unlike that of the Romans which preceded it, was a slow piecemeal affair and for more than a generation the invaders had been held back along the line of the Foss Way. Then the Anglo-Saxon victory here brought Gloucester, Cirencester and Bath under their control and split the remaining territories of their adversaries into the South West Peninsula and Wales. This old conflict, plus the evidence of Hinton Hill's Iron Age fort, the history of the Roman occupation and the site of another battlefield a short distance further along the route, all tend to confirm that this part of England has been

214

of strategic importance throughout our history.

The villages of Dyrham with its great house, Pennsylvania set on an exposed upland, and lofty Cold Aston, were passed by in turn as the Cotswold Way crossed the last part of Jurassic limestone country along my route. Then after descending into a deep valley, the path began a long climb back up to the top of Lansdown Hill near Bath.

On the right Freezing Hill, topped by a uniform line of trees, resembled, as I believe intended, the Royalist army which gathered here on 5 July 1643. Their aim was to capture Bath and so secure the western approach to the Royalist headquarters at Oxford. Lansdown Hill is a steep-sided flat plateau to the north of Bath and the Parliamentarians were ranged along its northern lip facing Freezing Hill over a deep saddle. The Royalists had to make several ferocious attacks up this steep slope before dislodging their opponents. The latter fell back to the next field wall, but by then the Royalists were too weakened to continue the fight. Under the cover of darkness the Parliamentarians retreated back to Bath leaving their camp fires and pikes behind to deceive the enemy. Both sides claimed to have won the battle, but the main objective, Bath, was never taken. The lone monument on the site is not a memorial to all those who fell but to a single man, one of the Royalist leaders. By such means are brave men remembered, or not as the case may be.

Then by way of Hanging Hill, Little Down Fort and Kelstern Round Hill, I finally arrived at Weston on the western outskirts of Bath, just as the sky was clouding over. The heavy rain came later, but by then that day's walk was over.

Between Bath and the Quantocks there was a stretch of countryside little frequented by walkers and, in addition, contained no convenient canals or long distance paths. So I was now totally dependent on the rights of way depicted on Ordnance Survey maps. From past experience I knew that these clear markings did not necessarily correspond to real paths across the landscape.

A stride along Bath's urban streets took me to Englishcombe, a small village on its outskirts, complete with stone dwellings, an attractive church and the remains of a small Norman motte and bailey castle. The name of the village at first struck me as odd because most English settlements were named long before the inhabitants of this country were known as such. The name of the next hamlet along the route, Inglesbatch, may have held a clue to its origins. Not only did 'Ingle' have some similarity to 'English' but Inga, Ingin, Ingel, Ingweald, and Ingeld were all old Anglo-Saxon personal names.

The nearby section of Wansdyke would probably have gone unnoticed if the map had not drawn it to my attention. But there it was in the form of a much weathered bank and ditch, first snaking into a nearby valley and then re-emerging and passing on into the distance. The purpose of Wansdyke is not known, but its Dark Age origins may indicate a temporary boundary between Britons and the encroaching Anglo-Saxons.

After a promising start, my way-finding soon ran into difficulties. I left Inglesbatch for Priston Mill along a clear-cut track signposted as Mill Lane. This ended abruptly at a small homestead from where three barking dogs emerged, the most aggressive of which advanced to nip my leg. A man and a young child, no doubt attracted by the racket, emerged from within and then stood watching the spectacle. When I called to the man to remove the dogs he replied that they were not his! After a delay, during which there may have been some second thoughts, he called the animals off, but no apology or explanation was forthcoming. It was the only incident of this nature on the whole 540 miles of my journey.

Continuing on, I was now aware that few, if any, members of the public used this right of way. All signs of the path had disappeared long before I came to broad Conygre Brook and, predictably, there was no bridge. As my timetable was tight I immediately attempted to jump across the stream and in the process very nearly fell back into the muddy water. As it was, I now had to put up with two boots full of the same. In a bad mood I then squelched across a meadow to Priston Mill, a large water-driven one which had been done up to attract car-borne tourists.

The long abandoned Somerset coal field began at Timsbury and here my surroundings became semi-urban. My lunch place was an abandoned railway track and later I passed a long row of terraced cottages which might once have been miners' homes. Then the sky clouded over and rain came pouring down. There was no trace of the path ahead, but I nevertheless took to the fields. After a considerable distance and many doubts, a blocked hand gate with a footpath sign upon it appeared ahead to provide reassurance that I was following the correct line of a theoretical but non-existent path. However, there was still a long way to go before a good stony track eventually took me out of these fields. Similar problems and bouts of heavy rain continued throughout that afternoon. Although the present surroundings were rather nondescript and semi-urban, some remaining rural features caught my eye. These included small odd-looking hills with lone trees on their summits and occasional buildings of lovely Bath stone. The day's walk ended at Chew Valley Lake where my wife in our car and I arrived simultaneously at a parking place occupied by twitchers, ice-cream eaters and nearby bird life.

The weather forecast for next day, a bank holiday, was appalling, predicting severe gales and very heavy rain.

My original plan had been to walk over the Mendips and out onto the Somerset Levels, but in view of this dire warning I decided to go only as far as Cheddar. An added factor in this choice was my lack of zeal following the footpath problems of the previous day.

From Chew Lake I initially stuck to roads and lanes, passing through West Harptree where many buildings were of mountain limestone, which hereabouts had a distinctly reddish hue. For the first time on my journey I was now moving onto an area of England's ancient upland. This village lay at the foot of the Mendip Hills, a name believed to have been derived from the old British word 'mynydd' meaning 'big hill'. Like its sister, the White Peak, there were no surface streams here and the slightly acidic rain water which drains through these rocks slowly dissolves them away. Over aeons in the Mendips this process has produced caves, ultimately culminating in picturesque rocky valleys of which Cheddar Gorge is the prime example.

With no signs of usable footpaths, I followed a road up and then across the flat plateau top where pastures were bounded by neat hedgerows and stone walls. However, these tidy signs could not hide the fact that this was a harsh countryside with only a limited range of flora, a character confirmed that morning by the omnipresent howling gale and a farm named Starve Lark. When I was beginning to think that no other living creatures were abroad, a young red deer trotted out onto the road immediately ahead. Suddenly becoming aware of my presence, it momentarily stopped dead in its tracks before scampering off down the highway into a gap in the boundary hedge.

Although farming could never have been easy up here, man had long been attracted to these hills by the metals which they contained. One of these mining areas was now nearby as the ground began to drop away into the valley known as Velvet Bottom. At last I abandoned roads for a clearly defined path which took me towards Cheddar. Remains of the old mining and smelting industry now lay around me in the form of disturbed ground, the ruins of stone condenser flumes and heaps of poisoned slag which nature has not yet been able to re-colonize. Further along at Charterhouse, the visible remains of the fort which the Romans built to protect their mining interests had been partly destroyed by later mining operations.

I had seen not seen a soul since first encountering the Mendips, but now I began to meet other walkers in increasing numbers. The path began to wind down a deepening, widening valley where signs of mining became less frequent and natural rock outcrops more dominant. The latter reminded me of the White Peak and my long gone youthful explorations in the company of good friends, for here shining outcrops stood above white screes and springy green turf. At Black Rock I crossed the road in the bottom of burgeoning Cheddar Gorge and joined a veritable column of pilgrims climbing up its eastern flank. The contrast between this place and those of up to an hour before could not have been greater.

On reaching the top of the hill, the sudden total exposure to the gale was momentarily overwhelming. It brought a flood of tears to my eyes and at first I had difficulty in maintaining my foothold. Finally, on becoming adjusted to these new conditions, I gave my attention to the surrounding scene. First came the vast, flat and very green panorama extending across the middle of the scene to a blue Bristol Channel. Then it was the turn of the nearby serried ranks of white cliffs falling away into the gorge. Finally, my eye was caught by the many distant hills and it sought out one in particular. The Quantocks appeared as a long grey shape along the southern horizon.

Immediately beyond their western end and partly obscured by a distant shower, I could just make out the hazy shape of Minehead's North Hill. After many long miles across the heart of England, my final goal was at last in sight.

It was a moment of great personal joy and I just had to share it with someone. A Welsh couple with a large collie stood nearby. They listened politely to my excited outburst, but made no response. From there the walk was downhill in more ways than one until I finally arrived at the crowds and flesh pots of Cheddar.

CHAPTER TWENTY TWO

ACROSS ENGLAND
CHEDDAR TO WATCHET

On this Sunday morning, the crowds had gone. So
Cheddar was peaceful apart from pealing church bells and
the sight of solitary figures making their customary
Sunday morning pilgrimage to the newsagents. The
threatening rain confirmed its presence, for on setting out a
torrent came tumbling down. But there was no wind so I
could put my umbrella to good use. For years I had
recognised their potential value, but as the walking
community did not use them neither did I. However, on
rereading George Borrow's 'Wild Wales', I noted that the
only possessions he carried with him on his travels were a
spare shirt, a pair of socks and an umbrella. There and then
I decided that what was good for George was also good for
me and I have carried a small brolly around with me ever
since.

The Somerset Levels lay ahead. My enthusiasm for
this next stage was not great, partly due to expected
footpath problems, and there were some, and partly
because I suspected that this region might be similar to the
Lincolnshire Fens, and it was not. However, the day did
prove a quirky one. The first part of the Levels, somewhat
to my surprise, consisted of small intimate meadows
bounded by tall hedges, a scene which bore no
resemblance to the Fens of my youth. Then, beyond the
River Axe, this flat land ended abruptly at higher ground.

From here I followed a lane which my map showed as petering out to become a public footpath. With my nagging concern about the condition of public rights of way in this region, when a middle-aged lady in working clothes emerged from a nearby dwelling, on impulse I sought her advice. It proved to be a mistake.

'Hello, does a public footpath continue onwards from the end of the road ahead?'

'Err, there might be one but I'm not sure.' Then after a short pause she added, 'Where are you going?'

'Stawell,' I replied.

This produced a chortle of surprise followed by 'You are going in the completely wrong direction.' In turn this was followed by 'When do you hope to arrive?'

'By four o'clock this afternoon.'

My latest response produced total disbelief and a dire prediction. 'You'll be lucky to get there by midnight at the earliest.'

With further discourse between a country walker and a modern country woman who went everywhere by car proving completely futile, I politely wished her 'Good Day' and went on my way.

In reality the path did not exist, but a nearby track, not a right of way, did head away in the same general direction. Unfortunately this led to some very muddy fields and then petered out. From here it took some time to get back onto a metalled lane. With the current slow rate of progress the lady's prediction of a midnight arrival could well have come true, so there and then I decided to stick to public roads. At first these led through hamlets on higher ground not far from Wedmore where King Alfred and the Danes had made the treaty which split England into its Anglo-Saxon and Danish regions. Then the terrain again dropped into the Levels. Here a substantial roadside drain, fringed by a line of pollarded willows, was joined by a succession of very full parallel ditches crossing flat grassy meadows. Again this scene was no reminder of the Fens, but it did stir memories of some of the older Dutch polders. But any likeness to the watery lowlands of my past was soon gone, for now the flat fields were no longer bounded by ditches but by high hedges of hawthorn and elderberry. A pattern of continuing change having been established, it was to continue for the remainder of that day. This change was not confined to the scene alone, as the weather also brought a succession of showers and constantly changing visibility.

There were few signs of humans around, but a surprise was awaiting on reaching the straight South Drain. Here, regimented lines of immobile seated anglers stretched away out of sight along each bank in a scene dominated by tall electricity pylons marching over the flats from the distant nuclear power station at Hinckley Point. During one interval of improved visibility, the long, low Polden Hills came into view for the first time. Following the day's odd pattern, nobody was in sight as I passed through the enlarged village of Chilton Polden. Beyond the dwellings a rare footpath led me through a meadow, where I received the unwelcome attentions of a skittish and probably very lonely horse. Then, on reaching the top of the hill, the former Roman road along its spine had now become the very busy A39.

Beyond the noisy traffic, I followed a winding lane down to the village of Stawell as the first sunshine of the day emerged from cloud. I had reached my destination half an hour before my wife was due to pick me up. In line with that day's oddities, the quiet village of Stawell displayed a most unusual sight. A solitary pony stood in the church porch, happily chomping away at a hay bucket.

The new morning was uncharacteristically fine and bright as I set out from Stawell. Being keen to reach the

223

delectable Quantock countryside as soon as possible, I followed lanes rather than face potential struggles with boggy tracks and paths which might eventually lead nowhere. From past experience in flat watery countrysides, I knew only too well that promising routes could tempt one on for considerable distances before finally ending at impassable waterways on three sides.

Striding along highways, I passed through the village of Chedzoy on the way to the River Parrett at Bridgwater. On this fresh, sunny morning Westonzoyland's elegant church tower, two miles away across the levels, stood out as a dark shape against the bright eastern sky. Near this village on 6 July 1685, Englishmen fought Englishmen for the last time at the Battle of Sedgemoor, where the poorly equipped and badly trained supporters of the Duke of Monmouth proved no match for King James's professional army. The slaughter at this site was bad enough, but the widespread execution of rebels which followed proved even worse.

The saddest aspect of this dreadful affair was that these sacrifices were made in vain because a short time later King James II fled from the country without a fight and was replaced by William and Mary.

The River Parrett at Bridgwater was not a pretty sight. Discoloured water, covered with animated swirls of green scum, scuttled past its greasy mud banks on an ebb tide. After passing beneath the M5 Motorway and crossing the River Parrett by a footbridge, I arrived at the buildings of this town and the Somerset Levels were now behind.

In line with my cautious mode of the day, I followed roads and then a lane up to the Quantocks. From a distance these appeared to be similar to the many lines of lowland hills that I had encountered since leaving Gibraltar Point in the spring. Then the glimpse of bright red soil in a nearby newly-ploughed field indicated that here was something very different.

I was now following one of those familiar long winding lanes across hills, which avoid unnecessary gradients, bypass villages and stand out from maps as possible through routes once used by foot travellers, horse riders and pack animals. These features often hint at ancient origins, from a time before present day patterns of settlement were established. Through long usage, this lane had dropped below ground level and its high banks were also fringed with tall hedgerows. So from here there were only occasional distant views and these revealed a Bristol Channel now grown into a wide blue sea, the twin islands of Steep Holm and Flat Holm seeming little more than a stone's throw away, and, most striking of all in that bright scene, the sea front buildings at Weston-super-Mare had taken on an exotic Mediterranean guise.

By early afternoon I emerged from trees to the delights of open moorland on Lydeard Hill, the sort of local countryside which I had come to love in recent years. Here, open rounded hills covered in heather and bracken fell away ever more steeply into secret, winding, wooded combes with little streams tumbling along their bottoms. By now the bracken on the upper slopes had become golden and the heather's purple had been replaced by a deep brown winter coat. Having seen no humans for some time, it was pleasing to find a few walkers up here, taking advantage of the fine weather. However, from the new wide scene it was obvious that this could not last. The sunlight was beginning to fade behind a high canopy of white cloud and along the western horizon a long dull mass was encroaching across the sky.

The Exmoor hills were again in view. So was Minehead's North Hill, much closer than when last seen from the top of the Mendips. Now it had the guise of a dark forbidding bulwark set against a leaden sea.

Nearby Wills Neck, the highest point of the

Quantocks, is a shapely heather clad hill unfortunately disfigured by a large quarry. A possible origin of its name is intriguing. The 'Wills' part is said to have the same root as the names 'Wales', 'Welsh', 'Cornwall' and, further afield, 'Walloons'. All derive from a Germanic word which means 'foreigner' or 'a foreign place'. The second part, 'Neck', could mean 'Ridge'. It is said that when the Anglo-Saxons first arrived in this area around AD700, they forcibly acquired the fertile lowlands and in the process despatched the native Britons to the hill tops. Then the incomers had the effrontery to describe the natives' place of banishment as the equivalent of 'Foreigners' Ridge'!

Only a brief rest was possible at Triscombe Stone, where Norman and I had cooked the first meal of that holiday in 1951, because the sky was now cloudy and the air cool. Down at the entrance to Quantock Combe, the air, as yet undisturbed by the fresh wind, still retained some residual warmth. A solitary, red hind was grazing in an adjacent meadow and, perhaps sensing my presence, this beautiful animal seemed ill at ease, periodically jerking her head up and looking around. Set against a bank of autumnal trees reaching up to open moorland, this lovely creature and its surroundings encapsulated my affection for this part of England. Shortly afterwards I celebrated my arrival on the south western moors with a chocolate ice-cream from the village shop in Crowcombe.

Two weeks later I was proceeding onwards from this village. The advance to winter had continued and now a cold north-west wind blew across a clouded sky. Above the rough bracken-covered pastures on the way to the tops, sudden exposure to the biting blast brought a stream of tears to my eyes and a persistent dewdrop at the end of my nose. All around the former autumnal colours had now become dull browns apart from the yellow dancing dried-out grasses of last summer. This was one of the many weathers which would have inspired the romantic poets Coleridge and Wordsworth during their sojourn at nearby Nether Stowey. I passed to the west of Dowsborough, a prominent hill covered by small hardy oaks which hide its large Iron Age fort. The Danes are the traditional local bogeymen and, according to legend, Dowsborough was one of several places where they were defeated.

Beyond the Bronze Age tumuli scattered along the ridge, I topped Beacon Hill, the last high point above the sea. During the Ice Ages much of today's Bristol Channel had been part of the Severn Valley. I had first seen the latter from a hill near Henley-in-Arden the previous June, but now on this October day the former river valley was a wide sea, full of white horses and surging breakers. While relishing the view, movement ahead and below caught my eye. The solitude was about to be broken by the arrival of a body of humans. Peripheral figures could be seen oscillating rapidly around its edge, like wasps disturbed from a nest, a sure sign that this was a party of youngsters. On meeting there was only a simple greeting between us, but in my mind I was transferring the pleasures of the hills on to them. They went on up to the open tops as I passed down into the conifer plantations below. The first trees were sickly, but lower down they had prospered, with the dark shade beneath their massed branches hiding a thick blanket of pine needles.

Ever since leaving the seashore behind at Cleethorpes on the other side of England, I had looked forward to reaching it once again. However, to get there I first had to cross a once extensive family estate, now with a variety of uses. A twisting lane led from the entrance lodge to a holiday camp on the cliffs above the sea. Here I hesitated. None of the camp's many signposts pointed out the way to the shore and my first attempt ended in failure among cliff top chalets and car parking places. Until now there had been no sign of other humans, but on my second attempt I was obliged to pass in front of the plate glass windows of a clubhouse. There I found myself looking at a large number of seated, well-dressed, mature ladies, demurely taking morning coffee. And, what is more, they were all looking at me. I scuttled off and, to my great relief at a children's play area, found a scruffy path heading down to the beach.

On reaching the open sandy, stony shore, all shelter from the weather had gone. Here successions of white waves, charging in from a very rough grey sea, sent clouds of spray and scud hurtling into the air as they crashed onto eroded rock platforms. It was a great moment. Scenes to landward at Skegness and this place, might have been very different from here but directly in front the gloomy skies, high winds and rough grey seas flecked with white were just the same.

The tide was coming in so I hastened around the base of the next headland onto the broad rocky beach leading to Watchet. Beyond the harbour walls of this old town Minehead's towering North Hill, now only eight miles away, stood out dark and severe against that day's leaden sky.

Watchet has had a long history of ups and downs. Its' early prosperity attracted the attention of Danish marauders who sacked the settlement more than once. Prosperity again came during the nineteenth century when high grade iron ore, mined on the nearby Brendon Hills, was exported from here to the steelworks of South Wales. Now the harbour's commercial trade has gone and the town's seaward side is increasingly threatened by the sea.

CHAPTER TWENTY THREE

ACROSS ENGLAND
INTO AND AROUND EXMOOR

Sunya and I stayed regularly at our holiday home in Watchet for a number of years. During this period we came to know West Somerset and Exmoor well, and also to love this little seaside town.

Then it was still a working port and I enjoyed watching cargo ships negotiating the tricky entrance to the harbour. The best known of its many seafaring sons over the centuries was John Short, otherwise Yankee Jack, a nickname which he acquired while serving on blockade runners during the American civil war. At home in Watchet he is best remembered as a fine singer who gave a large collection of sea songs and shanties to the doyen collector, Cecil Sharp

The following morning as I headed away 'from Watchet, the sky remained grey and the bitter wind still blew from the north east. St Decumen's, the parish church, stands on an inland hill top, and it was here in the graveyard that the fictional meeting took place between Coleridge's Ancient Mariner and the very patient wedding guest.

St Decumen's is one of several local churches dedicated to Celtic Saints. Although the Germanic tongue of the invading Anglo-Saxons replaced the old British language, the names and legends of many of these obscure old Celtic saints have survived. Apparently Decumen, accompanied by his cow, had set out by sea from Wales on, of all things, a wattle. His aim was to spread the Christian Gospel wherever he might land and he came ashore at Watchet. At first the natives do not appear to have been much taken with his ideas because one of them chopped his head off. The saint then picked up his head, washed it in a spring, which still exists today beside the church, and placed it back on his head. Thereafter it seems that his missionary work met with more success than before.

The path between this church and Kentsford Farm is the setting for another Watchet legend. A woman from Kentsford is said to have fallen into a deep coma which was mistaken for death and her body was placed in the family vault at the church. During the funeral service a greedy sexton saw the valuable rings on her fingers and decided to get them for himself. Returning at night with a lantern and being unable to remove the jewellery, he started to cut them away. This caused the lady's blood to flow and she returned to consciousness as the sexton fled in terror. The lady then made her way home along this footpath using the sexton's abandoned lantern to light the way. On arrival it appeared that she had great difficulty in persuading her husband that she was not a spirit. But all's well that ends well as she went on to produce a family line which still exists today.

After this Watchet information, I must return to my journey. From Kentsford to Washford, the way was along the bed of the old Mineral Railway which once carried iron ore down to Watchet Harbour. Cleeve Abbey ruins are close by at Washford and I was fascinated to learn that it was established by Cistercian monks from Revesby Abbey in Lincolnshire. From Washford a long footpath, probably another of those ancient packhorse routes, led to the top of Monkham Hill. At first arable fields lay beside the way, and it was here on a subsequent hot summer day that I encountered an unexpected nostalgic sight. A field of wheat had been cut, bound in sheaves and stacked in neat lines of stooks. I later realised that an old fashioned variety of corn had been grown and harvested in this fashion so that the stalks could be used for thatching.

Along the way I passed over the invisible boundary of Exmoor National Park. Having walked for hundreds of miles through soft, lowland landscapes, I now looked forward to crossing some wild country. My plan was to head westwards across the bleak moors before returning along the top of the high coast. Already arable ground had given way to rough pasture and at the top the wind blew cruelly before I could escape into the shelter of conifer plantations. Here, there was only a lone forester whose loud whining saw denied any interchange between us apart from hand waves. Then after dropping down to the head of the Avill Valley, I walked to Wootton Courtenay along a lowland path which twisted and turned delightfully across fields and meadows bound by hedges, trees and little streams.

Twelve days later I headed out from this village towards Exmoor's high tops. The overnight rain had ceased, but the sky still remained gloomy. At the start of the path, from Brockwell to the summit of Dunkery Beacon, the heavens opened up. My earlier doubts about the weather now seemed to be reinforced and I was not looking forward to a long exposed walk over the moors in bad weather. At the last of the sheltering trees before the open tops, the rain suddenly stopped. A little later, the clouds parted to reveal a small patch of bright blue sky and, encouragingly, it was just big enough to make one small sailor a pair of trousers. Then, on arriving at the summit of Dunkery Beacon, the sun came out creating a magical but short-lived moment. In the new crystal-clear light every soaking wet stone and pebble on the summit sparkled more brightly than diamonds can ever do. As the water ran away the sparkles faded, but for a brief magical moment I had enjoyed a very special Dunkery all to myself and it had been a great privilege.

The path continued along a broad heathery ridge to Dunkery's second and slightly lower summit known as Rowbarrows, named after a collection of Bronze Age tumuli. Then I followed paths and tracks along the boundary between the open moor and rough pastures. The new sharp sunshine turned the wet autumnal leaves of windbreak beech hedges into shining masses of copper. Here I met an elderly couple on a delectable wander over the moors to Badgworthy Water and Oare. They were the only walkers seen that day, and had my sights not been firmly set along the tops to the west, I might well have been tempted to join them.

Once more on open moorland, now predominantly grass covered, I encountered and then followed a track which had a marginally better walking surface than that of the surrounding moorland. Although now in poor condition, this feature still showed signs of purposeful construction. Later I discovered that it had been the route of a proposed railway that would have carried iron ore from inland mines down to the coast at Porlock. But the venture failed and the line was never completed. The rough ground surface was obscured by long coarse grasses, already limp and yellow at this season. So while concentrating on where my feet were going, I only looked up periodically to view the lovely, surrounding wasteland. Once I raised my head to see a deer and hind observing me quizzically from less than fifty yards away before they moved off unhurriedly over the skyline. All around yellow moors rolled away into the distance where sky blue alternated with piled white and grey cumulus clouds. At that moment I found it very hard to accept that this scene and others like it had once been despised as being unfit for either God or man.

Later the ground surface deteriorated into a bog where thick coarse grass hid a maze of dangerous ankle-twisting holes. More than once my boots were over-topped by this oozing mass. Although I had been walking on the moors for several hours, only now was I encountering them in their raw state. With eyes glued to the ground, a sudden noise and movement just beyond my field of vision startled me. A creature had leapt up from the long grass not more than three yards away. It was a large fox. Both of us were equally astonished, the creature because he had been fast asleep and I because my concentration had been elsewhere. This large animal, with a patchy coat and a brilliant ginger tail, at first appeared dazed but, collecting itself, loped away with measured stride and was soon out of sight.

At the end of that day I came to a well engineered highway which had been built across the moor in the nineteenth century, and followed it to a solitary place defined by cattle grids, gates, several prominent signs and a few parked cars. This spot was Brendon Two Gates on the Somerset and Devon boundary, masquerading as a frontier post in some faraway empty but very wet desert.

On returning next morning all other signs of life were absent. Momentarily, the bleak empty space of the high moor seemed totally alien after the cosy warmth of the car. Heading westwards I soon got into my stride following the stone-faced embankment marking the Exmoor Forest boundary before arriving at the present day lone Hoar Oak standing above the stream of the same name. Its first predecessor had been placed here by a Forest Tenant as a mark of respect for King Charles II. Apart from a few small trees on the nearby deserted farm, there were no others in the vicinity. A path now led up the valley to Exe Head, along the way passing below a ruined sheepfold which stood out like a tribal fortress high above the route. Back on the tops where the sky once more was huge, a watery sun had just managed to break through the grey.

Heading westwards again, I came to the infamous Chains, the place where the torrent which caused the disastrous 1952 Lynmouth flood fell to earth. At its top, the close-cropped, bright green grass of Chains Barrow stood out in stark contrast with the huge carpet of lank yellow mixed with dark brown all around. Always a lonely sinister place, its atmosphere that day was heightened by the now lowering clouds above. Others who have come under its spell include Henry Williamson, the author of 'Tarka the Otter'. He felt in touch with his ancestors here and also thought that it would be a suitable place for him to die. With no other living creatures in sight I did not choose to stay here long.

Nearby desolate man-made Pinkery Pond hid in a dip, and beyond there were barrows and the Long Stone, the largest surviving standing stone on Exmoor. The function of barrows as tombs is well known but that of standing stones remains conjectural.

After traversing many miles across heathery and grassy moors, I now left them behind for an enclosed track which, as the ground fell away, first led through rough pastures and then well tended meadows before reaching the village of Parracombe. The total peace of the moor had now been replaced by sounds of a distant barking dog, the clank of farm machinery and the steady hum of traffic on the main road.

From here, the route passed through a typical rolling Devon landscape of green pastures, high hedgerows, occasional woods and winding lanes. Dogs at the isolated farms came out barking, seeming unfamiliar with passers by. Yet, whenever I looked back, the high wild moors of that morning were nowhere to be seen, a circumstance common to moorland, but never to mountains. With the moors now no more than memories, my thoughts were already concentrating on the morrow when I would be wandering along an even wilder coast.

Rain had periodically threatened since morning and now by late afternoon the sky was again glowering. Stony Corner, an undistinguished crossroads, a mile from the coast not far from Coombe Martin, marked not only the end of that day's walk but also the most westerly point of my journey across England. On the next I would head eastwards along the coast towards Minehead.

Apart from one half day, I had walked alone from Gibraltar Point. Now I was joined for the last three and a half by Ken, my brother-in-law. We had first met in our RAF days and it was he, in a memorable moment of frustration fifty years before, who had tossed his inadequate boots away on snow covered Kinder Scout.

As Ken had been unwell, we delayed joining the Coast Path by walking along the lane from Stony Corner to Trentishoe Down. With occasional dwellings beside the road and the weather deceptively mild under the lee of Holdstone Down, our surroundings seemed benign. Then at the top of the road the wind suddenly caught us. Far below a wild sea, covered by white horses with their long manes streaming out behind them, crashed venomously onto dark rocks at the foot of the cliffs. By contrast, high above this maelstrom, steep, rounded, golden hills stood in intermittent sunshine and cloud shadow. It was a decade since I last visited this place and in the interim had all but forgotten its awesome majesty.

The South West Coast Path, which we had now joined, at first seemed intent on heading over the edge of a steep grassy slope into the briny, but at the last moment it veered eastwards along the top of precipitous cliffs. Following the seaward side of old enclosure walls high above the sea, we came to North Cleave Gut, a massive fissure in the cliffs where all the winds of the world seemed to have been funnelled. At its apex, the gale rising up from below made breathing impossible and all but blew us upwards off our feet.

Later, the wind moderated and we enjoyed a distant view of Lundy, an island at the boundary between the Bristol Channel and the broad Atlantic Ocean and, in the sharp light of that day, there was also a long panorama of the South Wales coast and hills. Then the path left the comforting stone wall on our right and headed out across an exposed windy, steep, slope to loop around prominent rocks hanging high above a turbulent sea. A large void appeared ahead. This was the deep Heddon Valley, heading straight inland from the coast. Its rugged seaward end is awesome, but inland the valley has a covering of gentle green pastures and trees. Following a steep descent we crossed the stream in the bottom and immediately began the long climb up its eastern bank.

There was not time to show Ken Heddons Mouth, where the river runs out onto a lonely beach surrounded by ferocious rocks and cliffs, and the only obvious sign of man is an old lime kiln once served by sailing vessels. Past travellers have likened this kiln to a castle guarding the shore and perhaps this is what it should have been. For a long time Barbary pirates raided this coast seeking slaves and booty and the beach was also used by smugglers. More recently it is said that crews of U-boats preying on British shipping during World War Two, surreptitiously landed here to replenish vital stocks of fresh water.

The first part of the climb from Heddon Valley was an attractive world of shelter, sun and warmth after our previous weather battering. So we stopped for lunch, spreading our belongings out over a bed of small rocks. Then the sun suddenly went behind clouds and it was as though all the light, colour and warmth of the world had suddenly been switched off. We did not tarry long and were soon enveloped in a heavy but short squall.

The high coast to the east was now in view. Beyond the tall waterfall, where Hollow Brook plunged towards the sea, we came to Woody Bay. Here, the few visible dwellings seemed all but smothered by trees. During the nineteenth century there were plans to convert Woody Bay into a seaside resort. Roads were laid out, some villas constructed as well as a tall steamer pier. Disaster was not long in coming. The jetty was badly damaged in a storm not long after completion, the project then failed and the promoter was sent to jail for misappropriating his backers' funds.

Later we came to Lee Abbey, never a proper abbey but originally an attractive house given that romantic name in Victorian times. Now it has grown into a conglomerate of buildings which despoil its lovely setting. After the thick tree cover had been left behind, a wider view of the heavens revealed ominous dark clouds with their undersides lit by remnants of a brighter sky out to sea. Then, at the Valley of Rocks, the black shapes of its pinnacles, set against this disquieting sky, reminded me of gloomy oil paintings of dramatic Old Testament scenes.

Castle Rock, the most impressive of these pinnacles, has a rough hewn path up to the top. It was constructed by an old man in the early days of Lynton's tourist trade so that he and his wife could dispense hot water and picnic provisions from a small hut at the top. This commercial activity ceased long ago, but the way to the top remains a great attraction for the large numbers who now come this way. On this lofty perch, the rocks, although massive, appear suspended in space and from it the views of land

and sea are spectacular.

A heavy squall arrived just as we were setting out along the North Walk, a broad near-level path constructed in the days when Lynmouth had been a popular resort for the rich. Here, without effort, those visitors could view distant seascapes, dizzy cliffs below and soaring rock pinnacles above. In Lynmouth that evening, I looked out of the bedroom window to find that the lights shining from buildings high above in the blackness had not changed over the years. Nor had the sounds of wind, rain and rushing waters in the river below.

The penultimate morning of my journey was again wet and windy, with grey clouds scudding across the sky and leaves falling in profusion. The tide was out, leaving a great fan of rocks below the river outfall. Halfway up to Countisbury the way passed below the massive bulwarks of Wind Hill, a large Iron Age fort. With the exception of one vulnerable quarter protected by a large earthwork it would have been near impregnable. Nothing is known about its ancient history, but a thousand years ago the Danes are believed to have suffered a major defeat here at the hands of the local Anglo-Saxons.

Rain came slanting in across the top of the hill and we dashed to the sheltered side of a small radio hut. Moving off too soon, a venomous wet wind caught us on an exposed col between two hillocks. Then, as if to make amends, a period of brilliant sunshine followed as we made our way across the steep face of part wooded, high hogsback hills falling into the sea. The high sea cliffs here in pre-Ice Age times were subsequently ground down to their present smooth, steep outlines during the subsequent very cold weather. In geological terms, the sea has returned only recently and so far has only eroded small cliffs at their bases.

A rhododendron forest led us into the Glenthorne

Estate, but on that day we did not see either its romantic Victorian Tudor House or the stony beach where, according to legend, Joseph of Aramethea, possibly in the company of the young Jesus, had stopped off while on their way by sea to Glastonbury. However, we could not escape a gloomy, tree-enclosed scene resembling a wayside burial ground, composed of a stone cross set on a dome of rocks. Behind the cross a water trough partly explains the Sisters' Fountain's name. It was given by Rev. Halliday, the founder of the estate in the early nineteenth century, to honour some of his family members. Two legends of uncertain veracity are associated with this spot. One was that Rev. Halliday made his decision to create the estate while pondering here and the other that Jesus, in the presence of Joseph, created this spring while looking for water after landing from the ship.

The next stage was along a track connecting scattered farms set on a sloping shelf of agricultural land in between the moorland and rough pastures above and a steep, tree-covered hillside falling into the sea below. All signs of the sun had now gone and the crowded trees and steep slopes around Culbone only increased the pervasive gloom. This former leprous charcoal burners settlement was very quiet as we passed through. Porlock Weir proved to be full of activity, no longer with coastal shipping and seamen, but with car-borne crowds who had come out here for an autumn weekend jaunt.

The final stage of my journey was short and momentous. The weather was very wet and windy, but fortunately the distance to be covered was relatively short and the gale would be at our backs. From Porlock Weir we headed across the seaward end of the Vale of Porlock, the first major gap in the coastal hills since leaving Stony Corner. Out on the shingle bank away from the shelter of the hills, the full force of the storm caught our backs.

Ducks, disturbed by our presence, took off from a nearby pond but were unable to make any progress against the gale. For us, muffled in our rain gear, we were only aware of pattering rain, the surging roars of the wind and the regular crashes of the sea on the other side of the shingle bank. As mentioned earlier, four years later this bank was permanently breached during another severe storm.

The buildings of Bossington at the far end of the bank provided all too brief protection from the weather. But I was able to show Ken the unspoilt thatched and tiled cottages, some with their large chimneys projecting onto the street. Many of these homes had been built before chimneys were commonplace. With open fires at their centres for both cooking and heating, and with the smoke drifting through the thatch above, living conditions would at best have been uncomfortable and grubby. It is said that when these new innovations first arrived, those who could afford them had them erected in these prominent positions to impress their less fortunate neighbours.

From here high ground, mostly open coastal moorland, led us to Minehead. Our next task was climb Hurlstone Combe, a steep narrow valley which acted as a funnel for the gale at our backs, continually trying to topple us forward. My original plan had been to follow the cliff top Rugged Coast Path, but as only a madman would have attempted it on that day, we crossed undulating moorland instead. Even so, we had a long way to go through gorse, grass and heather before the force at our backs lessened. Finally, wind ravaged trees announced the beginning of thick woodland on the approach to Minehead and at the first sheltered place we drank cups of hot coffee, while listening to, but no longer suffering from, the lashing storm. However we did not stop long because autumn cold soon began to penetrate our soaked bodies.

At Minehead's sea front we stopped at the signpost

marking the end of the South West Coast Path from Poole to Minehead via Lands End. It seemed as good a place as any to mark the end of my very different journey across the centre of England from sea to sea. My pilgrimage, 540 miles long, had taken me thirty-six and one half days to complete.

CHAPTER TWENTY FOUR

UP TO DATE

My long walk from Gibraltar Point to Minehead was an indulgence only possible on retirement from full-time employment. Even if the opportunity had existed forty or fifty years before, the problems in walking the route would have been infinitely greater. Since those days, the depiction of rights of way on 1:25000 and 1:50000 Ordnance Survey maps, the establishment of long distance footpaths, better waymarking, improved path clearance and a radical change in the national attitude towards countryside walking, have all been great boons. So have the absence of most deliberately blocked paths, intentionally misleading notices and unhelpful interference from aggressive landowners or their agents. Many of these changes have come from recognition of the combined economic and political impact of today's huge number of walkers. It is a salient fact, that on a long journey across England, my presence was only challenged once and that was by an aggressive dog. At one time I could never have imagined that this could be so.

I embarked on my long walk primarily for pleasure, but there was a supplementary objective. As stated earlier, prior to starting out I needed reassurance about the present condition of England's countryside. In the event I need not have worried. For someone whose concept of the country had recently become too coloured by its cities and urban life, it was wonderful to find so many miles of absolute peace along the way. In the past, towns and cities were small and almost all the country's population lived in villages where they spent their lives either working on the land or supporting those that did. Today the opposite applies. Few workers are now required for the present mechanised farming industry and, although the country's present population is far larger than before, for the most part it is crowded into large urban areas.

Rural change, which had been underway for a long time, was accelerated by the farming revolution of the last century which introduced mechanisation and widespread use of chemicals. During the second half of the twentieth century in particular, this led to a massive reduction in the numbers of working farms and farm workers. Many smaller farms were incorporated into larger ones and the long established large farms, which, when my grandfather was young employed up to thirty workers, now have only one or two employees. The true rural population of the countryside is now far lower than it was even after the depredations of the Black Death. On my summer walk across the centre of England, which admittedly avoided all conurbations as far as possible, the pervasive emptiness and loneliness of the countryside was also in part due to the current growing season, a time between tending and harvesting when noisy modern farm machinery was stilled.

Sometimes, depending on the weather, the terrain and the distance covered, walking can demand all one's physical and mental efforts and, at others, there is ample time for thought. This can range all the way from enjoyment of the surrounding scene to concern on darker matters. As a boy brought up in the countryside at a time when most farm work was manual, especially on smaller farms, I have seen the eradication of many back breaking jobs such as potato picking and boring ones such as hoeing, both of which occupied much of my school holiday time.

However, these economic improvements do have a worrying down side. When man first arrived here in numbers after the Ice Ages, the ground cover was mostly natural forest. Since then, to meet his own needs, he has gradually displaced natural growth by selective farming. Initially these developments, limited by knowledge and technology at the time, could be regarded as nudging nature along in a direction which suited man and this worked reasonably well for many centuries. However, in modern times, this largely unconscious strategy has changed to one of deliberate frontal attack. The consequences of this change are already painfully obvious to us in the recent loss of many species of flora and fauna and also in climate change with its associated severe weather and rise in sea levels.

A lifetime's walking has taught me that although nature can give us great pleasure, we always need to be wary of it. On one hand it is oblivious to our needs and, on another, can respond to our actions in surprisingly unexpected ways which might ultimately cost us dear. In ancient times man feared the world about him, but now he has come to believe that modern advances have given him complete control of the earth and everything upon it. This tenet is also coupled with the dangerous belief that only mankind matters. Nothing could be further from the truth. As an individual who has spent much of his spare time exposed to the great outdoors, I have not only acquired a great love for nature's gifts but am also keenly aware that this seeming friend can be a very dangerous enemy if not treated with proper respect. I sincerely hope that today's society as a whole will become similarly aware before it is too late to save not only our civilisation but perhaps mankind as a whole.

It is now a decade since I walked across England and,

partly due to reduced ability, there have been no similar ventures in the interim. However, while our walking may not be as vigorous as before, my wife and I still explore new haunts and revisit old much-loved ones both at home and abroad. In recent years I have gained great pleasure from Exmoor's wide-ranging beautiful scenes, which include both rugged and gentle coasts, lonely moors, wooded valleys, old fashioned farms and pretty villages. As in early days, I can now step directly from home into a lovely coastal world. From my current one, tree covered hillsides soon lead to open moorland standing high above the sea. Dunkery Beacon is also close by and in between there are many steep-sided, tree covered valleys. Even now I cannot claim to know Exmoor intimately as new corners and paths constantly surprise and delight me.

At the end of this account, instead of heaping paeans of praise on Exmoor as a whole, I will concentrate on one special path not far from my home because it demonstrates the essence of the region. The path's pleasures come from its scenery and from its' evidence of man's comings and goings in one small corner of our land. The Rugged Coast Path belies its name because it is no more than a rough route along the seaward edge of the hills topped by Selworthy Beacon.

From the west it is approached along the top of the coast leading eastwards from the head of Hurlstone Combe. Here, a mass of ground has slumped part way down to the shore, leaving a large grass covered shelf between the moorland and the sea. Far below, restless currents swirl continually off Hurlstone Point and nearby Selworthy Sands, exposed at low water, mirror this turbulence with regular deep scour marks across their surface.

Ahead lies East Combe, its bleak seaward entrance only softened once a year when heather blooms. Although this valley is only small, its size and that of the surrounding hills is deceptive because there is nothing here to provide a measure for the eye, and for this reason it is easy to imagine being among higher, wider hills in the north of the country.

On breasting the rise on East Combe's eastern flank, the path rounds a sharp corner above the sea and immediately heads into Henners Combe which is deeper, longer and less harsh than its neighbour. From here the path heads inland, crosses two small streams in the valley bottom and then climbs out in the direction of the sea. The inconspicuous lumps of concrete and rusty iron scattered in this valley are the minimal remains of a World War Two army tank training ground. Although nowadays difficult to visualise, a target trolley was once hauled backwards and forwards across the valley side as tanks, lumbering around nearby Selworthy Beacon, fired at it in turn. On reaching the seaward end of Henners Combe, the path turns right and passes onto the top of a steep slope some 650 feet above the sea and this extends eastwards for the next one and a half miles.

Ahead, dying and dead pines stand out against the sky. I have been told that their present and past sufferings are not due to their exposed position, but to lead poisoning from machine gun bullets fired into them more than half a century ago. Further along, a short section of path is always wet. The water comes from a spring higher up the hill which once met the needs of the people and animals at West Myne Farm. For centuries this settlement stood in an exposed but beautiful position where the gently undulating tops begin to fall away towards the sea. Although comfortless and lonely when cold winter gales came roaring in from the Atlantic, on lovely summer days the surroundings would have been beautiful, especially when the dominating blues of sea and sky gradually changed to gold with the approach of night.

During World War Two the farm's inhabitants and their stock were removed to make way for the battle training area. Surviving photographs show a substantial old house set in a slight dip in the landscape. The buildings were destroyed during the war and no humans came back, so cattle and sheep are now the only local inhabitants. Ironically, before the wartime road was built, access was along a rough track and out of necessity the old inhabitants had to be largely self sufficient. There is a tale, one hopes apocryphal, of a girl arriving at the farm as the farmer's new wife and only leaving it again in her coffin after mothering sixteen children.

Although the path is safe in fine weather, the sound of distant waves breaking on the shore far below wings up through the void to provide a sharp reminder of the true nature of this terrain. In one part, where there are vestiges of former trees, in spring this is still covered by dwarf bluebells which can cope with their exposed environment. On sunny days, the deep blue of this carpet vies with those of the sea below and the sky above. Later in the year, after the heather's purple has gone and the bracken has turned brown, small isolated rowans redress the balance of nature's fading colours with masses of orange-red berries. In another area, old landslides have left steep rocky hillocks, now recolonised by vegetation. Here, the presence of wildlife is sometimes confirmed by nearby sparrow hawks riding on the steady updraft.

The path eventually leads down into Grexy Combe, the largest wild valley along this stretch of coast. Each spring its upper reaches are covered with masses of yellow gorse and in early summer the bottom is carpeted with flowering orchids. The path then climbs a side combe and heads away across moorland to rejoin the South West Coastal Path. Here the remains of stone-faced boundary banks mark out long abandoned fields. Rearwards, a small Iron Age fort has now come into view on top of Furzebury Brake, a hill earlier overlooking the path. From this evidence it would appear that people lived up here for at least three millennia before finally departing in the middle of the twentieth century. This is only one small example of how much Exmoor has to offer and it is most unlikely that I will ever get to know the whole of it intimately.

Before ending I must say a few words about some very special mountains which first entranced me over half a century ago and have remained my joy ever since. They are the Lake District Fells, which for long have charmed, challenged and taught me, sometimes by salutary lessons, much of what I now know about mountain craft. In early days I always hastened to the high peaks with their steep rock scrambles. Now, having reached a more reflective age, I take time to partake of all that the region has to offer, which ranges from contact with gentle human scenes with their meadows, trees and stone dwellings, barns and enclosure walls, on to the broad lakes, dashing water courses and finally up to the bare glacier-sculpted tops. Each of these different very scenes has become emblazoned on my mind forever. I have always felt very much at home here, which might seem odd, bearing in mind the very different topography of my home region, but it could in part be due to their similar Scandinavian backgrounds.

In modern society where mankind dashes all over the world almost at whim and where distant places become less unique by the day, I rejoice that there is one small country which has everything from bleak, wild mountainous regions to flat, totally manmade ones. Moreover, each of these regions also has its own long and unique history. Finally, there is our wide-ranging rapidly changing weather, so the visual and physical impacts of the same scene on successive days can range from a sublime pleasure to a severe physical test. Thus, those who go walking could not experience more challenges, fascinating scenes and greater pleasures than the ones available near our own doorsteps.